BAKING
SOURDOUGH

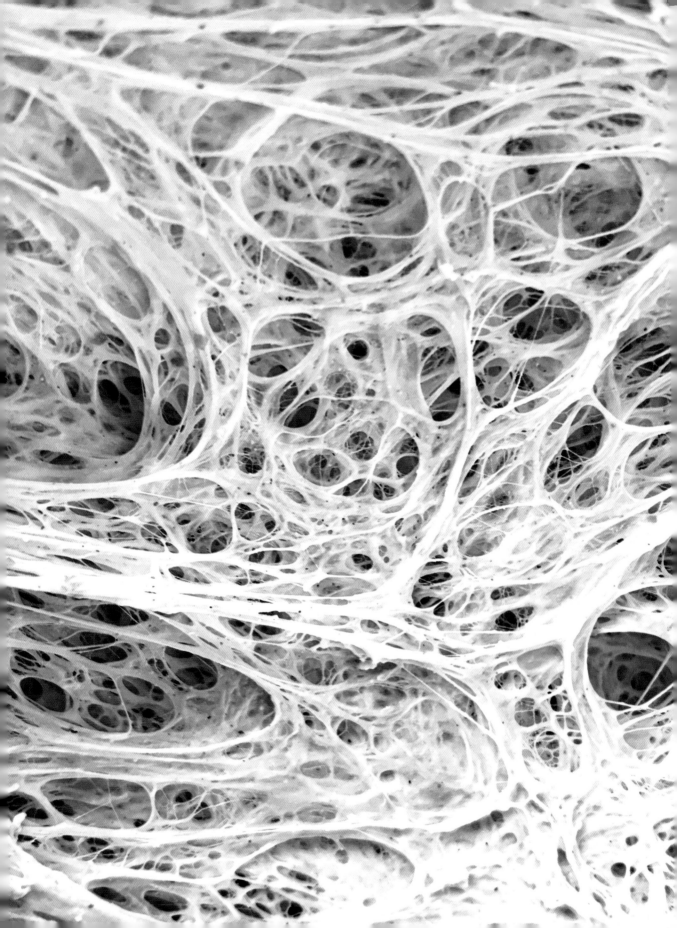

BAKING SOURDOUGH

Kevan Roberts

THE CROWOOD PRESS

First published in 2020 by
The Crowood Press Ltd
Ramsbury, Marlborough
Wiltshire SN8 2HR

enquiries@crowood.com

www.crowood.com

This impression 2020

British Library Cataloguing-in-Publication Data
A catalogue record for this book is available from the British Library.

ISBN 978 1 78500 683 8

Acknowledgements
I would like to extend special thanks to Crowood, for approaching me with the idea
of a book that suits my passions down to the ground, and allowing me to share my
knowledge with others.

The people at Wright's Flour Mill were exceptionally helpful in providing me with
insights into their industry, and opening my eyes to the story of the origins of bread.
Since the spike in my interest in milling, Komo have provided me with a home grain
mill, which has given me the opportunity to explore creating and developing my own
flours. My explorations have provided me with vital research to pour into these pages.

I would like to thank Bread Ahead for giving me confidence in the teaching
capabilities that have made this book possible. Thank you, also, to Helen Kilner, whose
pottery expertise was invaluable in creating the fermentation jars.

Many thanks go to my wife Kathryn, without whose patience I would not have made
it past my first draft. I would also like to thank my talented daughter Saffron, who
helped me so much to pull this book together and make sense of my ramblings.

The last acknowledgement goes to my darling mum Gladys, who taught me never to
give up on my dreams.

Typeset by Jean Cussons Typesetting, Diss, Norfolk

Printed and bound in India by Replika Press Pvt. Ltd.

CONTENTS

INTRODUCTION

This book will take you on a journey through the world of sourdough. It will follow the historical timeline of the development of this foodstuff through the ages, from its Neolithic birth to its near demise and consequent revival, as it played an integral part in the Artisan Movement. Despite a resurgence in the popularity of sourdough in recent years, it has not always been appreciated.

Baking Sourdough will show how sourdough is formed from natural yeast, and describe the intriguingly easy, and inexpensive, method that leads to such a highly developed sensory experience. It aims to bring to life the world of sourdough and enable all bread lovers – from professionals looking for ways of bulk-producing the same sour hit every time to amateur at-home bakers seeking bread's roots – to create their own sourdough, to their own specifications.

Detailed text and photos will help the reader to navigate the whole process of developing a sourdough, explaining various methods and giving a wide range of recipes to follow, in addition to providing a blueprint of how to adapt commercial yeasted recipes into sourdough. An exploration of different techniques will help to build confidence and knowledge, fully equipping the reader with the right tools for their sourdough journey. Also included is a full explanation of what a sourdough starter is and how to build the best one suited to the individual baker's needs – what to do if it goes wrong, how to look after it, and how best to maintain it.

Sourdough does not have to be a traditional loaf with a hearty crust. Sourdough croissants are a revelation, as is sourdough focaccia, ciabatta, and indeed the sourdough version of anything else that would otherwise be created using dried or baker's yeast. This book will enable you to be creative and encourage you to be brave. With a bit of experimentation, the results can be hugely rewarding. Step-by-step recipes will show you how to utilize sourdough in all types of baking. There is even a gluten-free section – sourdough is a sensory experience that can be shared by all!

There is a handy trouble-shooting guide at the end of the book. It is based on my years of experience of teaching people, either in groups or in one-to-one situations, and being bombarded with questions that start with 'What if…' or 'But mine…'.

What qualifies me to teach and write about this subject? I have been baking bread for over thirty years, and sourdough for around twenty-five. My journey started with leaving school in the mid-eighties with very little motivation or ambition. Coming from a mining village in the north of England during the miners' strike of Margaret Thatcher's tenure as Prime Minister, I had no real career direction other than wanting to be an actor. I was offered a job as a baker's apprentice in the local village bakery and took to it immediately. It appealed to me so much that, by the time I was in my early twenties, I had travelled around France and worked with vigour and interest in a bakery in the south of the country. It was here that I became completely captivated by the amazing breads created without baker's yeast! These breads were produced using what I could only describe as a grey sludge that lived in a big cast-iron bath. At certain times of day, it seemed to burst into life and bubble and grow. It was here that I came to learn that this was the 'real' yeast – the wild yeast that this bakery had cultivated for over

Close-up of a sourdough made with love.

forty years. Amazingly, until that time, although I had worked in bakeries for a number of years, I had not seen or baked with anything like it. It fascinated me beyond belief.

My baking expertise developed over the following decades as I managed a number of bakeries both large and small, both artisan and factory. The baking experiences were varied but the one constant was sourdough – I wanted to incorporate it into all manner of baking and spent a few years in New Product Development for bread, where I studied the process of creating a starter that could be managed en masse. The aim was to keep and maintain over a tonne of it at a time, but this just was not feasible. Despite many trials, sourdough is not yet ready for mass production on quite that scale. Perhaps every sourdough product should really be hand-crafted, with the baker feeling at one with the dough. My belief is that sourdough is not something to be mass-produced and packaged to go on the supermarket shelf alongside a thick square toasting loaf that will last for more than seven days.

My wife and I then took the brave decision to set up a bakery of our own. This is where I first made my own sourdoughs, ranging from Marmite sourdough rolls to sourdough pain au chocolat. I loved it so much that I spent around eighteen hours a day perfecting my craft. We very quickly grew into a wholesale supply bakery that also taught bakers and novices alike how to bake bread. It was during these years that I fell in love with teaching – sharing my knowledge,

Perfecting my presentation techniques in the early days of my sourdough discoveries.

enthusiasm and passion for all things bread, and in particular sourdough. An increasing desire to share my knowledge brought me to the world-renowned baking school in Borough Market in London, England, where I now teach across five days a week to around 130 people. About half of them are sourdough enthusiasts, while the other half are new to the wonders of the world of sourdough and fermentation. Hopefully, my wide-ranging experience and knowledge will help to guide you on your own sourdough journey, whatever that may turn out to be.

CHAPTER 1

THE HISTORY OF SOURDOUGH

The history of sourdough is, in fact, the history of bread. Any discussion of the origins of bread itself must involve a consideration of bread's roots within sourdough.

WHERE DID SOURDOUGH COME FROM?

The first question to be asked is, 'Where did sourdough come from?' What is it that makes sourdough the original, and most natural, process of bread-making? It all comes down to wild yeast.

Wild yeasts are organisms that live everywhere. They thrive in the atmosphere, in water, on human skin, and in the air that is inhaled by people every single day. When wild yeast organisms encounter water and flour, a fermentation process begins. The organisms combine with the natural sugars and starches within the flour, in conjunction with lactic acid bacteria. Once the lactic acid and wild yeast come into contact, they both fight to survive and grow into that ecosystem; the by-product of this is carbon dioxide. The carbon dioxide produced then generates the prove in the dough, by expanding the space that the dough takes up. This process, on a basic level, also creates the sour 'bite' in the taste of the resulting bread. Although the science behind sourdough is essential in the creation of its unique taste, the at-home baker does not need a complete understanding of it, in order to use it to enhance homemade bakes.

With this chemical reaction, the history of sourdough began. However, researchers can only speculate as to the exact time when people began using wild yeast cultures to generate volume in the breads they produced. What is now known, though, is that experiments with grains as a food source have been taking place for longer than people originally thought. As recently as 2009, Julio Mercedear, an archaeologist working for the University of Calgary in Canada, and his team, whilst excavating grinding stones, found the residue of sorghum (a gluten-free flour) still embedded within them. These finds were hidden deep within the caves around Mozambique; on closer examination, it was determined that they pre-dated even the

Wild yeast in the making, cultivated in a Kilner jar.

Historic kisra flatbread.

Agricultural Big Bang, being around 100,000 years old. It seems that, technically, gluten-free is not the new phenomenon that people perceive it to be.

The shift from man being a hunter-gatherer to being a farmer happened sporadically around the globe. Each continent naturally selected its own indigenous seeds to harvest. These ancient grains were **spelt**, mostly farmed around central Europe; **khorasan**, from Iran, Afghanistan and central Asia; **emmer**, Europe and Asia; **rye**, central Europe; **millet**, Africa and south-east Asia; and **sorghum** in Africa, India and Nigeria, to name but a few.

The first breads were, undoubtedly, unleavened flatbreads. These were made using only flour and water mixed into a porridge-like paste, then poured on to a heated stone to bake. The Sudanese, to this day, still make a flatbread with sorghum flour and wild yeast, known as kisra. The Ethiopians produce another

Flatbread in an outdoor tandoor oven.

flatbread, with teff flour, called injera, using a similar process to that of the Sudanese kisra, but with the aid of fermentation (using wild yeast). A similar outcome can be achieved by baking the flatbreads on a large river rock outside on a wood-burning fire, and the results can be remarkable. This process enables the baker to enjoy the unmistakable aroma of the bread baking, and to embark on a multisensory journey involving the palette – something that has to be experienced to be believed. Sadly, the introduction of the enclosed oven has removed this vital piece of the jigsaw from the whole experience of baking fermented breads. This is one of the few developments in the history of sourdough that could be interpreted as a regression. Although the change from open to enclosed ovens has allowed mass production, and the development of timings, structures, and so on, it is a must for the modern baker to try the old, open method. It provides another level of understanding of the impact of different baking processes on flavour – something that is not always considered.

WILD YEAST

Although there is no definitive answer as to why using a wild yeast culture in breads started, it is possible to make an educated guess. As human beings planned and organized their lives, they inevitably looked at making more food than was necessary simply to give sustenance for a few days. Unwittingly, in doing so, they discovered that leaving bread mixtures aside for several hours, if not days, would allow wild yeast to permeate the dough. The result was an increase in the volume of the breads. With this came much-improved textures and taste and, overall, a more palatable product.

One of the oldest sourdough breads to be excavated, in Switzerland, dated back to 3700BC. The Ancient Egyptians also discovered and recorded the use of leavening by means of a wild yeast culture. Hieroglyphs showing the production of bread, and even a few bread recipes, were often accompanied by images depicting the brewing and consumption of alcohol. Clearly there was a link between the two processes as long ago as 3000BC.

THE HISTORY OF BREAD (AND BEER)

The Earliest Beers

The history of beer is linked to the birth of civilization. It was discovered as soon as our ancestors decided to settle down. The earliest evidence of Man drinking beer is found in a pictogram on a seal dating from the 4th millennium BC. Discovered in Tepe Gawra (in modern Iraq), a settlement in ancient Mesopotamia, it shows two figures drinking from a large jug through straws. Of course, what they are drinking would have been quite unlike the beer of today. It was more like a soup – a blend of water and grains – and it would have been swimming with chaff and other impurities, which is why it was drunk through cane straws. Beer also appears on the oldest written testimony of human civilization – the tablets from Uruk in Mesopotamia (also in modern-day Iraq). The beverage was represented in Sumerian script by a jug crossed by two parallel lines. Archaeologists have also found many tablets containing lists of names, accompanied by the inscription 'issued his daily ration of beer and bread'. These 'payrolls' are the source of a great deal of information about our ancestors' diets. As writing developed, the symbol representing beer became more abstract. This can be seen in the cuneiform script, which is a precursor of the Roman alphabet.

The beer revolution began, as might be imagined, where the agricultural revolution began, that is to say, in the region known as the Fertile Crescent. This was an ideal location for founding settlements and cultivating wheat. Our ancestors discovered that grains tasted better when pounded and mixed with water, and that they were even more palatable when the water was heated. Shortly afterwards, they discovered another of wheat's virtues – it could be stored for months or even years without losing its nutritional properties. The ancient civilizations began to construct storage houses for their grain and attached greater importance to the harvest. They also invented tools, including sickles, woven baskets and quern stones for grinding, which made their work easier. With these developments, they bid farewell to the constant fear of starvation that had caused them to lead their migratory lifestyle. From

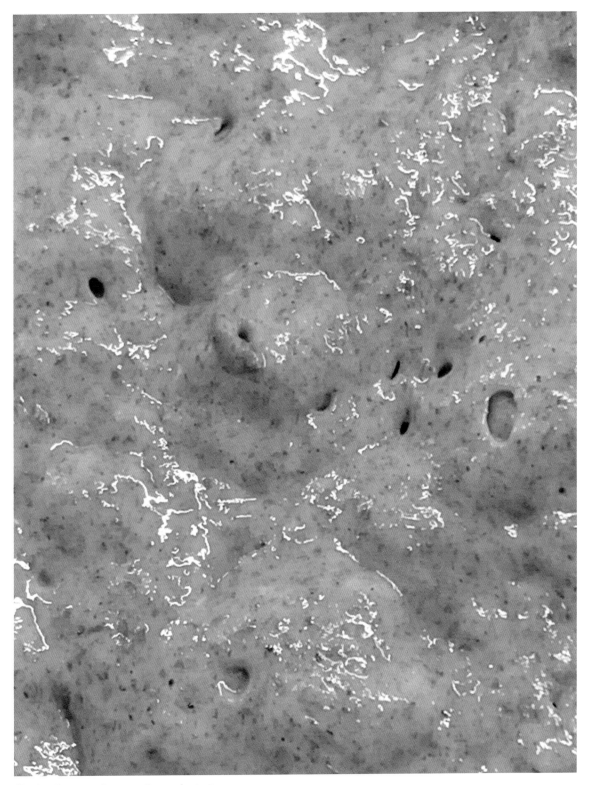

The developmental stages of an early starter.

this point onwards, men and women were able to settle down and start keeping watch over those grain storehouses.

As time passed, it became clear that grain soaked in water would begin to sprout and take on a sweet taste. (Today, it is known that this is caused by amylase enzymes, which convert starch into maltose.) This is how malt came into being. When left to stand in water at room temperature for a few days, it begins to fizz and, when drunk, it can trigger a pleasant state of intoxication. Of course, our beer-supping ancestors did not know the science behind the process – under the influence of yeast that could have existed naturally in the air, sugar ferments and alcohol is created. After beer had been discovered, people learned through trial and error that the more malted barley they added, and the longer it was left to ferment, the stronger the drink became. Ancient brewers also observed that, if the beer was brewed in the same vessel, it was better. This of course happened because there were residual yeast colonies in cracks in the vessel, so fermentation occurred more swiftly.

One theory claims that beer is older than bread, positing that the first cake, the great-grandfather of bread, was created from spilled fermented beer, which was then dried and baked on a hot stone. Beer in those days was a watery mush created from saturated fermented grains, so, although it has never been confirmed, the theory will surely strike a chord with every beer drinker.

Most of the information we have about the history of beer has been left to us by two civilizations who used writing systems – the Sumerians and the Egyptians. Interestingly, beer was drunk by a group of people from a single jug using a long straw, even when individual vessels were available. Clearly, beer drinking already had a social aspect – it was a ritual and a manner of sharing provisions. The state of intoxication following the drinking of beer also had its mystical aspect in many cultures. Beer was believed to be a gift of the gods. The Egyptians claimed that it was Osiris, the protector of crops, who one day created a mush from water and sprouting grain. Being busy with other matters, he forgot about it and left it for a few days in the sun. When he returned, he saw that the drink had fermented, and he decided to drink it. The god felt so fantastic that he decided to share his invention with people. The Egyptians often used beer in religious ceremonies, as well as during funerals and festivals associated with agriculture.

We have the Sumerians to thank for the earliest example of world literature, the *Epic of Gilgamesh*. It contains the story of the bestial giant Enkidu, who, after drinking beer, 'washed his body and shed his fur so as to become a man'. In Mesopotamia, knowledge of beer and bread was something that separated civilized people from those who were 'wild'. The Egyptians left us the inscriptions in the Pyramid Texts of the rulers of the 4th and 5th Dynasties. They not only used writing to describe mighty deeds, but also mundane trade transactions. In fact, beer is the most frequently mentioned foodstuff in these early examples of writing. Beer was basically a currency that was also easily divisible. Records show that, during the construction of the pyramid complex at Giza, the workers got four loaves of bread and around five litres of beer a day. 'Bread and beer' naturally became a symbol of wealth. When the Egyptians become reputable brewers, they began to export their beer around the world.

Beer was also recommended in Egypt as a medicine and as a base for other medicaments, and it was regularly prescribed for both women and children. It was indeed healthier than the alternative – it contained fewer micro-organisms than untreated water from the Nile, because it was partially composed of alcohol. In addition, during its production process, the water was heated to a relatively high temperature. This was usually done by heating stones in a fire and throwing them into the mix.

Bread and Beyond

Agriculture, combined with the milling process to make flour, created the building blocks to form a new civilization. The change to agriculture took a huge amount of organization and care; farming was not a one-man operation, but a team effort, with people coming together, each with his or her own individual role to play. However, with progress and efficiency, it became possible to produce more than each settlement of people needed for their own use. As a result, members of civilization began to develop into traders. This required some form of written record for stock levels and growing seasons, as well as maths, for calculating volume and yield. In addition, some form of currency was needed to trade with. As the traders began to achieve success, a divide between the affluent and the poor developed, and there came a need to protect the assets of the wealthy. The natural progression was to form the first armies.

Settlements developed their own different trades – field workers, millers and, essentially, bakers to bring the product of their toil all together in the bread. Those settlements evolved into villages and towns, then cities, with bread production playing a vital part in building the societies in which we live today. A number of archaeological discoveries have proved the historic influence of this valuable food source. Large bakeries excavated alongside the Pyramids of Ancient Egypt would have helped to deliver the large intake of carbohydrates needed to sustain the building workforce, again reflecting the significance of bread. Easily transported and easily stored, with an extraordinarily long shelf life – when kept in the correct conditions – grain has been vital for many centuries to ensure that people have not gone hungry.

'The Sour Doughs'

In the 19th century, Gold Rush prospectors came to California to make their fortune. These bands of brothers, just like the Egyptian workforce, needed food that provided them with energy-releasing nutrients – a good intake of carbohydrates was important. Fortunately, the Gold Rush migrants were aware of how to create bread from a wild yeast culture. According to anecdotes, the prospectors would even sleep with their cultures, keeping them nice and warm, to encourage fermentation. A sourdough starter has always needed devoted care and attention; in California, it was crucial to the survival of the prospectors. If their starter died, they would lose their main source of carbohydrate – and thereby their main source of nutrition. Caring for the starter could be a matter of life and death.

The prospectors quickly earned the nickname 'The Sour Doughs', after their breads. In the second year of the Gold Rush, 1849, the Boudin Bakery was opened in San Francisco by Isidore Boudin, son of a master baker in France. The bakery continues to thrive today, still producing a world-famous (and trademarked) product known as 'The Original San Francisco Sourdough'. According to local bakers, sourdough bread made outside a 50-mile radius of San Francisco tastes different, less sour. Tests carried out in the 1970s on the lactobacilli bacterium, a major player in the success of a sourdough, concluded that it was indeed special. It had not yet been catalogued, so it gained the name *L. sanfraciscensis*. However, it later turned out that the bacteria were not quite as unique as first thought and can be found in bakeries across France and Germany.

YEAST

Wild yeast was king for thousands of years, until brewer's yeast came flying on to the scene. Even before Louis Pasteur's advanced methods of culturing yeast gave the world a better idea of the fermentation process, a Dutch distiller in 1780 started marketing yeast foam to bakers. It was made by skimming from the top of fermenting alcohol. The process was refined by a Vienna factory in 1867, which removed the yeast foam, filtered it and dried it into compressed cakes. In 1872, the Vienna Process, as it was known, was developed by Charles Fleischmann into an active dry yeast.

The production and development of yeast was moving fast. It was a godsend for bakers and allowed production to move forwards, enabling bakeries to create and produce on a vast scale. Commercial active yeast was fast and reliable, and, with Fleischmann's development, there seemed to be no need to go back to a wild yeast culture.

MOVING TO MASS PRODUCTION

Human beings are impatient; always striving for a better and easier way of doing things; maybe this is why humanity has been so successful, evolving from hunter-gatherers to farmers, and building a civilization on grain. The milling process went through many advancements. From the prehistoric method of grinding the seeds into flour with a rock, via the rotary quern (dating from around 300BC, the Romans took milling to another level around the 1st century AD, building the Barbegal water mill in France, which could produce 4.5 tonnes of flour a day. Farming methods were also developing rapidly. Originally, agriculture was hugely labour-intensive, requiring time and financial investment, but, with the introduction of steam, machines could replace horses to do the bulk of the work. This, along with the introduction of crop rotation and pesticides, enabled farming to become faster and more cost-effective.

Once the Industrial Revolution came along, the ensuing scientific developments moved the industry closer to the holy grail of bread: a bread that bakers had been striving for since first hitting a rock on seed. The one final component that would make this a reality finally appeared in the 1960s, when the British developed the Chorleywood Process. This allowed the mixing of dough at a high speed, and the inclusion of a combination of extras such as Vitamin C, emulsifiers and enzymes. Bakers could use lower-grade flours and the industry could now make bread from start to finish in just three hours. The same process is still used today in mass production. It was a massive revolution and played a significant part in bringing down the cost of bread for the consumer. The downside is that, in the speeding-up of the process, the fermentation period has been significantly reduced. This is the part of the process that allows the dough to build flavours. It is time-consuming but crucial in the development of the taste of the bread.

The dream of mass production had become a reality, and the world's industrial bakers could revel in the appearance of such products as 'Wonder Bread', as American white sliced loaf. Gone were the sour undertones and the chewy textures – but also gone was the flavour! The masses had spoken and they had chosen convenience and cost over flavour. In the mass-production industry, this type of product was not even given the name of bread; instead, it was known as a 'sandwich carrier'. The name says it all; this

bread was no longer a source of nutrition and taste, but merely a vehicle to transport a filling from plate or packet to mouth! And nobody was mourning the death of sourdough – the death of a depth of flavour to bread. The new generation of breads were hailed as hygienic, pure and healthy. The product was promoted as an energy builder, and even as an aid to weight loss! The original combination of flour, water and yeast had made so much progress, but it had lost so much along the way.

THE ARTISAN MOVEMENT

In the 1970s, questions began to be asked about the health claims made by 'Wonder Bread', and rumblings were beginning in other quarters too. World-renowned French baker Raymond Calvel voiced his concern about the dire quality of bread in France, while the American writer Henry Miller famously wrote that 'you can travel 50,000 miles in America without tasting a piece of good bread'. In 1974, Edward Espe Brown published a revolutionary book entitled *The Tassajara Bread Book*. Written by a Zen Buddhist teacher at the Tassajara Zen Mountain Center in California, this book offered its readers a more soulful approach to bread-making. It returned to older methods of making and baking and re-introduced the main component: wild yeast! During this period, independent mills also started to pop up, among them Bob's Red Mill, in California, which was established in 1978 by Bob and Charlee Moore. Bob Moore's driving force for healthier options started with the death of his father as the result of a heart attack at the young age of 49. The first mill opened in Redding, California, and was at the forefront of a seismic change around California, where people were looking for a healthier way of living. The Artisan Movement was now in full swing, and many great bakers took up the baton: Peter Reinhart, Chad Robertson, Lionel Poilâne, to name just a few.

The Artisan Movement sought to return to the older methods of bread production, using starters, sponges, poolish and pre-ferments, along with old dough. The aim was to get back the flavour that had been missing from mass-produced breads, and the truth was the Movement was able to come up with much better results than had been achieved prior to the Industrial Revolution. By the 1970s, bakers had gathered more information about the power of pre-ferments and such like, and were developing much better-tasting breads; and this time it was out of desire, not necessity. The classic French pain de campagne was one bread that was developed in the booming 1970s, while ciabatta first appeared in 1982, produced by a baker from Verona, who wanted to create an Italian rival to the mighty French baguette. Although it is relatively recent, many believe ciabatta to be an ancient bread, perhaps because, with the intense specificity of its flavour, it clearly has its roots in the old methods.

SAFEGUARDING SOURDOUGH FOR THE FUTURE

Man's history and relationship with bread runs deep. It seems that there is no other food source that stirs up as much emotion. When there is a shortage of bread products, the public are not happy; there have been countless bread riots around the world, and it has even played its part in revolution! Mistakes have been made by the baking industry, but lessons have been learned and the industry is now looking back to the past for inspiration. Society has changed and increasing numbers of consumers now want integrity, traceability, health and taste. It represents a big shift from a culture

Example of a historical pre-ferment.

Birth of the milling process.

of convenience and low cost. After all that history and development, bread is now in the best place it has ever been when it comes to sourdough. The flavours are back, and the structures have been perfected. We are now closer than ever to the original method of enhancing the taste of bread, whilst having progressed a long way in terms of our understanding of how to develop it.

Sourdough has become so important to the world of baking it now has its own sourdough library. Created by the Puratos company, it is dedicated to the conservation and promotion of sourdoughs from all over the world, and aims to secure the survival of the biodiversity of strains for the future. It started off with forty-three sourdoughs and now comprises eighty-four. Every year, attention is focused on one country or region in particular. As many different sourdoughs as possible are collected, then Professor Marco Gobbetti analyses their composition for micro-organisms in his laboratory. More than 700 strains of wild yeast and 1,500 lactic bacteria have been recorded to date. The library is a non-profit initiative. It is Puratos' way of contributing to the wonderful world of natural ferments and the technology of fermentation, while guaranteeing the safeguarding of bakers' sourdough.

Starter after a feed.

CHAPTER 2

SOURDOUGH STARTER

This chapter will examine the science behind the process of combining flour and water. In addition to this, it will demonstrate various ways of creating a sourdough starter, using different flours and a variety of additions, as well as just flour and water. It will outline which flours are most suitable for a consistently reliable starter and explain why this is the case. It will also take the reader step by step through the process of building a starter, using photographs to illustrate each stage of the magical process.

THE INITIAL MIXTURE

So, in terms of the science, what exactly is happening in the flour and water mixture? Many people fail with sourdough, simply because they do not understand the fundamentals when it comes to the starter. Almost as soon as water encounters flour, an enzyme already living in the flour starts breaking down the starches within it, converting them into sugar. This enzyme is called **amylase**. It is also found in human saliva and is what initially breaks down starch molecules in carbohydrates, long before they are fully digested. Once the flour's amylase has developed sugars from the starch molecules, wild yeast and bacteria then begin feeding on these natural sugars, and this eventually creates the sour taste.

Wild yeast (*Saccharomyces exiguous*) lives all around: in the water, on fruits and seeds, and in flour. This is where there may be some confusion, particularly when people attempt to grow a starter from fruit. It is the natural yeast attaching itself to the fruit, trying to penetrate the fruit to gain access and feed upon the natural sugars, not the fruit itself that is of interest.

Wild yeast is easily visible on a bunch of grapes, as the powdery substance surrounding each grape. Wild yeast and commercial yeast are cousins that create similar developmental results but behave very differently. The commercial yeast has a pH of 5.4, whereas most sourdoughs have a pH of around 3 to 4. Simply put, this means commercial yeast produces more carbon dioxide than wild yeast, resulting in a faster prove

Flour in a glass jar.

time. Wild yeast has a slower prove, due to its slightly more acidic nature, although the extra time to develop wild yeast is hugely made up for in additional flavour. ***Lactobacillus*** **bacteria** now creeps in and competes with the wild yeast bacteria to devour the natural sugars. *Lactobacillus* is a non-harmful bacterium present in cheese and yogurt; the by-product from the lactobacillus feeding on the sugar is **lactic acid**, which gives the sourdough that deep flavour, as well as **acetic acid**, which gives it the unmistakably sour hit. Meanwhile, the by-product from the wild yeast feeding on the sugar is carbon dioxide, which creates the rise. This entirely natural amalgamation makes the perfect micro-environment to build a sourdough; it truly is a beautiful thing.

So why not just use commercial yeast if it is faster than wild yeast? The trouble with this symbiotic relationship is that it is a little one-sided. The lactic acid outweighs the yeast and slows down the production of carbon dioxide; conversely, wild yeast seems to be more tolerant of the acidic concoction, in comparison with commercial yeast. During the making of sourdough, the acid has more time to attack the gluten molecules, due to the longer proving time. This is something that ought to be avoided, because the gluten matrix is what is holding this perfectly natural marriage together. If the gluten chains break, all the carbon dioxide will escape, and what will be left will resemble a kisra flatbread – delicious, but not quite the desired result. In sourdough, most of the gluten has been pre-digested by the lactobacillus bacteria, which is beneficial. Having less gluten in bread stops the bloated feeling that some people can experience after eating breads that are higher in gluten. Clearly, the extra fermentation time makes a sourdough loaf a much healthier option than the standard supermarket 'sandwich carrier'. Additionally, sourdough has a much longer shelf life. One ingredient in the recipe for a supermarket loaf is vinegar, which is included because its acidity helps to kill off the mould spores that ordinarily spoil this kind of bread. Sourdough produces its own acidic levels that work better at keeping the mould at bay, for much longer. There is no need for vinegar additions in these natural loaves.

HOUSING A SOURDOUGH STARTER

A starter immediately needs to be stored in specific conditions. Its home must be a manageable size (but able to hold more than 700g), easy to clean, and permanent; this new member of the family, just like a human being, will find moving home stressful. Most of its life will be spent residing in a fridge, so it should have a spot dedicated to it. The next consideration is how pleasing to the eye the starter's receptacle needs to be while the starter is waiting to be used? As soon as it becomes active (and make no mistake, this *will* be an exciting time!), you will want to do what society has done for hundreds of years to record proud moments: take a photograph. There is a strong possibility the starter may even be introduced to the world of social media.

A Kilner jar is a good choice. The starter is always clearly visible, which will allow you to observe its growth and development and to quickly determine its general health. The jar will be easy to keep clean, in case the starter begins to overspill; just one top tip: remove the rubber seal! Starters produce carbon dioxide constantly, and they are not very conducive to being locked in a jar with no escape route. If this were to happen, a new starter would need to be created.

A good Tupperware tub is equally good – see-through enough to see what is going on inside, and easy to keep clean.

A further option is a fermentation pot, a vessel created purely for the purpose. It has a water seal moat around the rim so that, as the starter commences its fermentation process, the gasses that are produced gently pass through the seal. This gives the starter a more rhythmic fermentation and prevents unwanted air entering the starter's atmosphere.

Location and environment are crucial to building and maintaining the perfect starter. Lots of different strains and factors come into play during this process. Each one is totally unique, and each starter takes on and adapts to its particular environment. Try making several starters and placing each one in a different environment during its building process, to see which conditions work best for you.

A fermentation pot; a potential home for a starter.

A glass Mason ball jar makes a good starter home.

THE STARTER

Names and Terminology

Starter, sourdough starter, levain, starter sponge, mother sponge, biga, chef, poolish…. There are so many names and so much terminology when it comes to sourdough, it is useful to have some understanding of the meaning and differences between them all.

All these names refer to types of pre-ferment: a mixture of flour, water and leavening agent (such as yeast), combined in advance of making a bread dough. In the pre-ferment, the water hydrates the flour and the fermentation reactions begin. The pre-ferment is a head start for the dough. Using one makes the dough easier to knead and adds flavour to the bread.

The different names developed in different locations. For example, 'poolish' supposedly originated in France, where Polish immigrants introduced the idea of a pre-ferment. 'Levain' seems to derive simply from the

French term for starter. Some say that 'sourdough starter' is specific to the starters created on the West Coast of the United States. Some use the term 'starter' for the part of the mixture that is kept, and 'levain' for the part that is mixed up to use in the dough; others use 'storage leaven' for the keeper and 'starter sponge' for the part that is used. 'Chef', 'mother' and 'primary levain' are also used to refer to the part that is kept. And some people say the mixture changes names throughout the bread-making process. As long as everyone involved in the process of creating a particular sourdough knows what each stage is being called, then it does not really matter!

Pre-Ferments

Pre-ferments can be sorted into two main categories:

1. Pre-ferments made with commercial yeast, which are mixed about a day before the dough is mixed, and used entirely.
2. Pre-ferments that contain wild yeasts and bacteria, which are maintained and then increased when needed for bread, and used over and over. This second type of pre-ferment is what will be referred to as the sourdough starter.

A closer look at the second type of ferment is useful to understand some of the science of sourdough. A sourdough starter is created by mixing flour and water, and then allowing the micro-organisms – wild yeasts and bacteria – that live in the flour and air to thrive and multiply. Over time, a stable population of these micro-organisms develops. When used in bread, the micro-organisms perform fermentation reactions, producing the gas that makes the dough rise and the molecules that give it flavour. These flavour molecules are different from those produced by commercial yeast.

Variations in sourdough starters can change the flavour of the resulting bread. Despite the name, not all sourdough breads have a sour tang. Time, temperature, and the presence of various types of bacteria can all affect the final flavour:

- **Time:** a sourdough loaf baked the same day it is mixed will have a milder taste than one that has had a longer fermentation time. Some bakers even recommend using less starter in the recipe to extend the time it takes the dough to rise.
- **Temperature:** different rising temperatures affect the activity of the yeasts and various types of bacteria, resulting in differences. According to Francisco Migoya, head chef and co-author of *Modernist Bread*, proving at cold temperatures (by putting the dough into a fridge overnight) generally results in a harsher acidic taste. On the other hand, letting the dough rise out of the fridge results in a more mellow acidic flavour. Many bakers use a combination of the two temperatures; it is worth experimenting with rising temperatures until you find the flavour you like best.
- **Wet vs dry:** different starter consistencies will produce different results. A wetter starter, which looks more like batter than dough, is more reactive, while a drier, dough-like starter is better for storing for longer periods in the refrigerator.

DAY 1: THE BIRTH OF THE STARTER

Flours

There are a variety of flours available to build the starter. In theory, a starter can be built with any flour, but tests show that the most versatile and reliable starters are built on wholewheat, rye and spelt.

Rye flour seems to be a good choice, as it ferments more quickly than wheat flour and is packed with starch just waiting for the amylase to convert it into sugar. Rye is a grain that originated in Turkey but is now mainly grown in northern Europe. It is suitable as a winter crop due to its being much hardier and easier to grow than wheat or barley. As for going organic, the jury is still out, but sourdough does lend itself to a more naturalistic approach to bread-making, so it would seem a natural choice. Why would someone living as healthy a lifestyle as possible, growing and eating organic fruit and vegetables, opting to make their own bread using their own home-grown wild yeast, use a flour that was not organic? The real enthusiast might even consider growing the grain and milling their own flour, using a small hand-held milling machine. One alternative to going this far is to find a local miller of organic rye and use their flour, thus reducing food miles in the process.

Water

The choice of water can affect the starter. Tap water contains chlorine and this could upset the harmonious balance of the mixture. It is advisable either to boil and cool tap water before adding to the starter or to filter it; there are many water filters on the market, some of which are attached under the sink to filter at the tap. There are tablets that are immersed and, over time, do the same job, or you can simply buy the best local spring water and use this.

The recipe on page 28 is an example of a basic starter using a rye flour.

Flour and water being weighed out for a starter in a glass jar.

Finished starter, alongside the beginning of a fresh sourdough.

STARTER WITH RYE FLOUR

Ingredients

Light rye flour	50g
Water	50g

Equipment

Fermentation container of choice to hold up to 700g of finished starter
Tea towel, linen or muslin cloth
Finger (not a spoon)

Method

1. Before creating the starter, wash your hands, but do not sanitize, as there are valuable wild yeasts at your fingertips. Put your chosen vessel on to the scale and choose the unit (grams). Tare the scale (reset to zero).

2. Scoop the 50g of flour, using your hand, into the vessel. Tare the scale again, then weigh the water out to 50g, on top of the weighed flour.

3. Now, using only one finger, stir the mixture to make it into a paste. (Using a finger increases the chances of introducing more wild yeast into the mix.)

4. Cover with a damp clean tea towel, making sure to keep the starter out of direct sunlight. The tea towel

will prevent the starter from drying out, retaining the moisture that is essential to the bacteria's survival. It will also stop things falling into the starter, whilst allowing good bacteria in.

5. Choose where the container will reside for the next few days of its maturity. The surroundings will make a difference to the eventual outcome of baked products made from the wild yeast. For example, site it under a lemon verbena for a slightly lemon tang; leave it on the side in a kitchen where lots of cooking takes place daily using garlic and strong-smelling spices and this will, believe it or not, permeate the starter through the cover. It is at this stage when individual experiments can be interesting. If there are two people in the household who are interested in sourdough, why not make two starters? Perhaps one is a fastidious hand-washer while the other takes a more laissez-faire approach to cleanliness. One starter might be left in the kitchen and the other under a highly aromatic plant, such as lavender, lemon verbena or jasmine, or a herb, such as rosemary, thyme and coriander. You might also want to name the starter at this point. The reasoning behind this is unclear, but it is however a practice used by most bakers who bake sourdough.

• •

DAYS 2 TO 6: THE FEEDING PROCESS

On the second day, take the tea towel off the top of the starter, pop the pot back on to the scale, and tare again and again. Using hands only, add 50g of the same flour used on day 1, along with 50g of water. Stir to combine it using a finger and then return it to its resting place, simply replacing the damp cloth on the top.

Repeat this process daily until day 6. It does not have to be done at the exact same time every day, however, it really ought to be around every twenty-four hours, otherwise the starter will get very hungry. Try to stick to at least a similar time of day – perhaps every morning when you have breakfast, or every evening before retiring. It will be easier to remember to feed the starter if the job is attached to part of your daily routine.

There are a number of signs to look out for when feeding the starter. Depending on the environment, there may be some activity in the form of air bubbles, which indicates that the fermentation process is happening. Sometimes this is seen by around day 3, however, it will depend on the temperature of the room. The time of year is fairly important – a consistent room temperature of 21°C is ideal to increase and encourage the production of yeast. It is well documented that yeast, as bacteria, thrive best in humid conditions, so the starter should not be left in a very cold room. Perhaps the ideal time of year to grow a starter is early summer/late spring, depending on where you live.

Other things to look out for include a black watery sludge on the top of the starter; this is an alcoholic by-product known as the hooch, and is a good indicator that the starter is hungry. If it has already run out of its food source at this early stage, it will be because it has become too warm. In this case, it needs to be moved to a cooler location. At this stage, the best living conditions for the starter's development are vital. Too many people, when the hooch appears, conclude that this is the end, give up and throw the starter away. However, all is not necessarily lost. There are two schools of thought: some say tip all the hooch down the drain, and others prefer to leave it all in. One compromise is to dispose of half of the hooch and then stir in the remainder with the next feed of flour and water. This can be done earlier than the twenty-four-hour window if hooch is noted.

DAY 6

Once it has arrived at day 6, the new starter can reside in the fridge if it is not to be used daily. If, however, it is to be used on a daily basis, it is best kept out at room temperature, but in this case it will need to be fed daily, as warmth will promote fermentation and hunger. Placing the starter in a fridge at a temperature of around 5°C stops this process in its tracks and temporarily confuses it, giving it a feeling of satiation.

This will stop it being hungry, but it will need a food source around once a week or it will die. If it is to be moved to the fridge, take off the cloth and replace it with the vessel's lid. This will prevent other aromas from the fridge seeping into the starter.

DAY 7 ONWARDS

At this point, it is a good idea to log feeding days and times. After the initial building phase, a starter will need feeding once every week to two weeks, if it is not being used. If a sourdough is not going to be produced for a month or so, the starter still needs feeding. If it is not feasible to feed it during this time frame – if you are away from home, for example – there are a few options available:

- Date and freeze the starter. It will lie dormant in the freezer, where the cold will stop fermentation completely in its tracks, but not so much as to be irreversible. To aid recovery from a deep freeze, as soon as the starter has defrosted, give it a feed as usual, but add a drop of honey to the feed and give it a good stir. This will give the starter a sugar rush.
- Find a trustworthy and reliable friend – probably the same friend you ask to water your home-grown vegetables when you are away. It is not worth risking losing the starter you have so lovingly cultivated. Your sourdough-sitter needs to know that this is a living organism, because if it is not fed properly, it will fall ill and eventually die. You might want to gift this person some starter early on, to ensure that they know how vital it is.
- Ask a local bakery whether they would be prepared to look after and house your starter in your absence.

If the starter is not to be used right away, there will be an abundance of starter dough. A good, healthy amount to keep as a stock is 500g (remember, the home for the starter should hold a volume of 700g). If it grows beyond this weight because it has been fed and no baking with it has taken place, there are a few options:

- The first, and most obvious, option is to get baking!

- Encourage friends to take up sourdough baking and gift them some of your fully activated starter.
- Dry out your starter indefinitely. This is a process that is adopted by all good bakeries, so that they have a back-up in case of disaster.
- The fourth option is to throw part of your starter away down the sink. This is the one you most want to avoid, so hone your time management skills and always be aware of your stock levels.

To dry out your starter, take it out and spread a thin layer over a piece of parchment paper with a spatula. Place the paper in the oven with just the oven light left on; this will give it a gentle heat to aid the drying process. Leave it in the oven overnight (do not be tempted to speed the process by turning the oven on, because this will kill the yeast (which dies at around 140°C. On the next day, take out the paper and lift off the dried sheet of starter. Break it into pieces and grind them in a pestle and mortar, then transfer into a Ziplock bag. This is also a great way to post starter to friends.

To rehydrate the dried starter, weigh it first, as a certain amount of weight will have been lost during the drying process in the oven. Do not go on the starting weight. Second, weigh out the equivalent in water and dissolve the crumbled mass of dried starter into this. Add the same amount of flour as you did water, then leave out overnight, covered with a cloth not a lid – this is important in the regeneration process. To guarantee revival, it is a good idea to add a level teaspoon of honey, to give the starter a sugar boost for the yeast bacteria to thrive on. Again, the room temperature should be around 21°C. The next day, use 50g of flour and 50g of water; two days of feeding should be enough time for a full recovery.

A HEALTHY STARTER

Right from birth, the starter is trying to find a good, harmonious living environment. In the early days and weeks, this can be unpredictable and it can become over-active, giving clear indicators by way of its fermentation activity and the production of hooch. Ideally, it should be living out of direct sunlight and in a temperature of 21°C. The environment must not be too warm, as the yeast will die above 60°C.

In order to health check a starter to ascertain whether it can be revived, first have a look at it. Does it look bad? Is it dark, crusty and mouldy? If so, unscrew the lid to have a smell. In seconds, the vile pungent smell will be unmistakable. If it smells like rancid nappies, it is definitely dead, and beyond repair.

The bakers at the Boudin Bakery in San Francisco claim that their starter dates back to 1849, while a woman in Newcastle, in the north of England, believes that hers is 120 years old. With proper maintenance and the correct environment, your starter will outlive you. It has the capacity to become a family legacy, but, like all living things, it must be cared for.

Fully active wild yeast starter, ready to go!

CHAPTER 3

FUNDAMENTALS AND METHODS

Once a starter has been built, you will need to consider your list of equipment, the pre-ferment options available to make using a sourdough starter, and how to craft a basic sourdough loaf.

EQUIPMENT

You will need the following equipment to hand to make your sourdoughs.

Weighing Scales

Baking sourdough will involve using small weights, so a digital scale that registers 0.1 grams is best. Go for a flatbed scale, not one with a bowl already attached. Small battery digital scales are best for home use. For micro/small bakeries there are the larger more industrial ones that are plugged in and charge a battery at the same time. This allows the scales to be used next to and away from a power source.

Mixing Bowl/s

It is best practice to have a few mixing bowls in different sizes. The plastic clear ones are lightweight, easy to stack, easy to see through to ascertain how much the dough has proved, and fairly flexible. They are also cheap to replace, and less likely to break if dropped than a beautiful ceramic bowl.

Measuring Jugs

A jug may be used for measuring liquids, although most bakers measure by weight, not volume. That said, many recipes do indicate volumes, so a 2-litre jug clearly marked with ml will be useful. Do not choose

A suitable mixing bowl.

Measuring jug for the initial starter mix.

one that measures every 100ml – more units will give a more exact measurement.

Proving Baskets

Proving baskets come in all shapes and sizes, including the bâtard, the boule and even a triangle. Sourdough can take twelve to twenty-four hours to prove and the proving basket gives the dough much-needed support during this time. The shape that is chosen is purely down to personal choice. For a long bread, which is ideal to use sliced for bruschetta, choose the bâtard. For a simpler, traditional round loaf, choose the boule. This is an excellent option for serving soup the French way, particularly French onion soup. Simply cut the top off the loaf and scoop out the bread, leaving a bowl to fill and bread to dip.

LEFT: **Spring onion sourdough examples proving in baskets to a perfectly rounded structure.**

Stacked proving baskets in various shapes, for different styles of loaf.

Proving baskets in various shapes.

Stacked proving baskets.

Couche Cloth

Traditionally made from sturdy linen, the couche cloth is a great aid to proving baguettes. It is laid flat, heavily dusted with flour (preferably rye flour), then gathered or ruched to provide a series of 'valleys' in the linen. The baguettes are placed in the valleys, with the sides of each one cradling and supporting the dough during its final prove. A decent linen tea towel will do the job just as well, but is not quite as authentic. Sourdough dough usually has a higher level of hydration than ordinary dough, as well as a lengthy prove time. As a result, if it does not get enough support, the dough will spread. A baguette baking tray is also good to maintain form in the oven and to help keep a row of baguettes uniform.

Temperature Probe

A probe is a great aid in finding the right dough temperature. The temperature of the dough as it begins proving, or rising, affects the rate of fermentation and, in turn, the flavour and texture of the finished product. The optimal temperature for most bread doughs is 75°C. To arrive at this temperature, it is not usually possible to manipulate variables such as the temperature of the room, flour or starter (if it is being used). Instead, professional bakers use a simple mathematical formula to calculate the temperature of the one variable they can control: the water. This formula also considers the amount of heat generated by the mixing method. Hand-kneaded doughs have a friction factor of 5°C, while the friction factor of a stand mixer is 20°C, and the very vigorous action of a food processor produces a friction factor of 25°C.

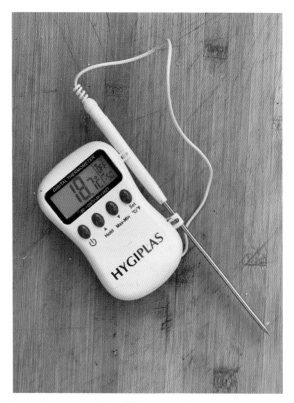

A temperature probe will help you to be as accurate as possible.

Essential dough scrapers will enable smooth and easy movement of your dough.

To calculate the ideal water temperature, multiply the optimal dough temperature of 75°C by 3 (multiply by 4 if the recipe includes a starter), then subtract the temperatures of the room, flour and starter (if applicable), and the friction factor from this figure. For example, for dough kneaded in a stand mixer (friction factor of 20) when the room, flour, and starter temperatures are all 71°C, the required water temperature would be 67°C:

$$(75 \times 4) - 71 - 71 - 71 - 20 = 67°C$$

Dough Scraper

For shaping and moving dough around, go for a plastic scraper that will bend with the dough. It should be flexible enough to run around the inside of a bowl in order to bring together all the dough before tipping it on to the kneading surface. A dough scraper can also be used to cut dough in half, scrape loose dough from a work surface, and many more things besides. Do not be fooled into believing a strong expensive metal one is needed; it is not. By all means buy one, but do purchase a plastic one as well.

Baker's Lame

A baker's lame is a must for getting the perfect designs on the top of loaves. It is a curved razor blade, held in its curved position with either a wooden or plastic handle. It enables the baker to score the dough at the correct angle, giving both a score and a lift in one motion. They can cost from £3 to £15, depending on quality. If you are not yet ready for this investment, buy ten razor blades in a chemist's or supermarket and thread them on to a wooden coffee stirrer. This will give you ten lames for about £1.50! They will need to be replaced regularly if you are baking many loaves, as a good slash cannot be made with a blunt blade.

A lame is used to score patterns into a loaf.

Water Spray Bottle

Water sprayed in the base of the oven will generate steam, which helps to create a golden crust on sourdough. The spray bottle will also come in handy for applying egg wash or water if an alternative finish to the dough is required – for example, attaching seed toppings or creating artistic stencil techniques. They can be purchased very cheaply from most hardware shops.

OVENS AND BAKING

There are many types and models of oven, all built and behaving differently. Temperatures and times mentioned in recipes should be used as an indication only, and will need to be adjusted according to the workings of each particular oven in order to achieve the best baking result.

Temperature, Thermostats, Steam and Stones

An oven can make or break a carefully prepared loaf, so it is wise to be aware of any quirky traits of your particular model. If you do not own a professional bread-baking oven, but you want to achieve similar results using a domestic oven, the following tips on temperature, thermostats, steam and stones might be helpful:

- Get to know your oven. How accurately does it indicate the temperature? First of all, it is wise to find out what the real temperature of your oven is, compared to the temperature indicated on the settings. You can do this by using a 'true temp' oven thermometer.
- If the heating system is too close to the bread (in other words, if your oven is quite small), the top of the loaf could burn. You have to adjust the temperature, or make sure that the oven temperature is turned down after about ten minutes, so that the elements stop increasing their heat. The closer the top of the oven is to the bread, the more heat will get transferred faster, which means quicker browning and potential burning.
- Introduce steam in the oven to allow the dough to expand at the beginning of the baking process. The steam will keep the outside moist and gelatinous. While the inside of the bread will want to expand under the heat, it will not be kept back by a dried-out outer shell. This is known as oven spring.
- Release the steam at a later stage of the baking process to allow the crust to form. If the moisture is retained, the crust will stay soft.
- If steam is not used, the surface of the loaf will dry out in minutes. Oven spring, which usually occurs 5 minutes into the baking process, will not really get a chance this way; for this, the bread is in the oven together with the steam, with the oven door being closed very quickly to make sure the steam stays in. One common method is to put a tray in the bottom of the oven, put the bread in the oven, then pour hot water on to the tray and quickly close the door so that the steam is trapped.
- To create maximum steam, it is also possible to put a metal tray on the oven floor and fill it with some 'sauna'-type stones (hot stones that do not shatter easily) or a heavy chain. After ensuring that it can withstand this type of use, preheat the oven, then put the bread in and carefully pour 100ml of water

Dutch oven.

Complete sourdough in a Dutch oven.

into the tray before quickly closing the oven door.

- Another option is to spray the oven walls with water, as long as the oven will not be damaged by this. Electronics, oven window and ceramic walls can all suffer damage from water or sudden temperature shock. The simpler the oven, the fewer parts there are to become damaged.
- The introduction of a large amount of cold dough will cause the temperature in a normal household oven to drop quite a bit. A pizza stone in the oven can create more thermal mass.
- The workings of a stone oven can be simulated by starting the baking on a high temperature (250°C) and then lowering the oven temperature ten minutes later to stop the browning, whilst continuing the baking of the bread. The higher starting temperature will give a better oven spring.
- A domestic oven can be used as a proving cabinet by preheating it for a minute to 25–30°C and then turning it off before putting the dough in to prove. We do this with our small stone oven, which retains the temperature for a long time because of the stones and isolation. We like to prove our croissants in this manner.
- If you are not satisfied with the baking results from your oven, try creating an 'oven in an oven' by using a cast-iron pan (Dutch oven) or a cloche, if your oven can accommodate this. The lid of the pan or cloche traps moisture rising from the dough and creates the steam that produces a crusty loaf with a creamy crumb (the bread's interior). Make sure you preheat the oven and pan together.

Baking Outdoors

Making and baking sourdough outdoors is highly recommended. It just feels like the right environment for this activity – a fantastic multisensory experience that will reconnect the baker with nature. It is well known that being among the elements and taking in vitamin D and fresh air can improve an individual's mood and mental health. Indulge your biophilia – your innate human affinity with nature – and see your productivity and creativity surge. Getting out of that poorly ventilated building, with its damaging build-up of carbon dioxide, will certainly reduce feelings of fatigue and stress. Eating outdoors is also often associated with an occasion – a family BBQ during the warmer months, a picnic in the park, or fish and chips by the sea are all special events, when the food seems to be perceived with greater excitement.

To experience all these benefits, you can buy or build your own outdoor oven. These come in many different forms, from homemade clay and brick ovens to purpose-built models. If time and building experience are not assets you possess, then the latter may be worth considering.

The Kamado grill is a good all-rounder that will satisfy all baking requirements, including the high temperature that is necessary for an authentic sourdough pizza – this oven can reach 500°F. It also has a pizza stone, which is ideal for pizza, sangak and flatbreads or, with the aid of the Dutch oven, a boule can be created.

A medium-scale outdoor oven.

ABOVE: **Baking outdoors with a Kamado grill.**

An outdoor oven in Morocco, similar to a wood-fired pizza oven

Flatbreads cooking on heated walls.

STORE CUPBOARD ESSENTIALS

The following are the items you will most likely need for the majority of the recipes in this book. They all have a fairly long shelf life, so it is a good idea to keep the store cupboard stocked up and these ingredients to hand:

- Strong white bread flour.
- Rye flour.
- Wholemeal flour.
- Spelt flour.
- Honey.
- Sea salt or table salt. This is down to personal choice. Sea salt is a pure product, while table salt contains added iodine, which can maintain a healthy thyroid. They both contain a similar amount of sodium by weight.
- A starter that is at least six days old (this is a fridge item, not a store cupboard essential).
- Disposable plastic shower caps – great alternative to cling film to cover the bowl to aid the prove.

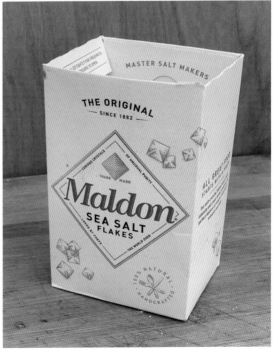

Cracked sea salt.

A large pinch of cracked sea salt.

Rye flour.

PRE-FERMENTS

Now you have a starter and the equipment and ingredients that you need, you can begin to consider pre-ferments. A pre-ferment is a great way to get ahead of bakes and helps with the time management of making a sourdough bread. There are a number of versions from which to choose: biga, sponge, poolish, stiff starter…. These names may seem alien to a novice in the world of sourdough, but they are simply differently named pre-ferments that mean the same thing. A pre-ferment is started the day before bringing a bread recipe together, thereby giving the baker a head start. It is a combination of the starter, flour and water, which allows the fermentation process to begin in advance, giving all the flavour and a better structure to the final dough. The following guide to pre-ferments will point you in the right direction of which pre-ferment to use, depending on the required results.

Completed starter resting in a Kilner jar.

Fundamentals of sourdough, from the starter to the formation of gluten structures (*continued overleaf*).

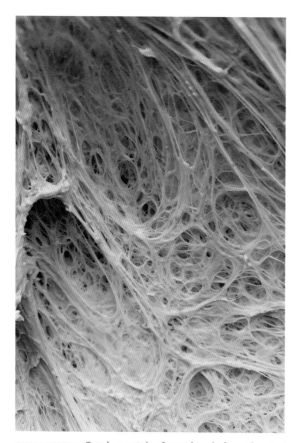
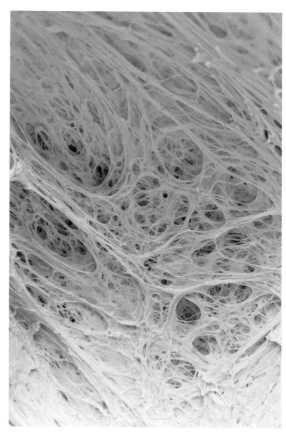

ABOVE AND BELOW: **Fundamentals of sourdough, from the starter to the formation of gluten structures** *(continued).*

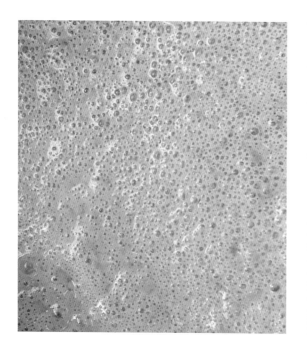

BIGA

The biga starter is Italy's take on a pre-ferment. It usually includes a small percentage of baker's yeast, but if the baker's yeast is exchanged for the starter, it is just the same as a stiff starter. The biga/stiff starter gives a subtler sour flavour and works well when added into a pain au levain or miche pugliese.

Ingredients

Bread flour (of choice)	100g
Water	60g
Sourdough starter	30g

Method

1. Dissolve the starter into the water using fingers to achieve a milky consistency.
2. Add to the flour and combine. This will feel stiff and quite tricky to bring together with the low hydration. If making a large batch, it is advisable to use a mixer.
3. Once combined, cover and leave overnight at room temperature (if the room temperature is above 17°C, leave the mixture out for one hour, then move it into the fridge overnight). Once it has fermented, it will be nice and vibrant and ready to be combined with different ingredients, to have its flavour further enhanced.

· ·

POOLISH

A poolish pre-ferment is used in many breads and is the preferred choice of the French baker. It was first used by the Polish bakers around 1840 and was brought to France around 1920. There is a common saying amongst bakers: 'If in doubt, use a poolish!'. It is great to use in baguettes and is an excellent addition when baking an authentic Italian pizza.

Ingredients	
Bread flour (of choice)	100g
Water	100g
Sourdough starter	30g

Method

1. Dissolve the starter into the water using the fingers, achieving a milky consistency.
2. Add to the flour and combine; this will be easy do, with the high hydration.
3. Once combined, cover and leave overnight at room temperature (if the room temperature is above 17°C, leave the mixture out for one hour, then move it into the fridge). It will ferment overnight and will be nice and vibrant, ready to go into a recipe the next day.

· ·

Poolish pre-ferment.

· ·

SPONGE

A sponge is usually a combination of flour, water and starter with the addition of eggs, butter, sugar and milk. A sponge is mostly used to make enriched doughs for baked goods such as brioche and panettone.

Ingredients	
Bread flour (of choice)	100g
Water or milk	45g
Sourdough starter	30g
Egg yolk	32g
Butter	32g

Method

1. Dissolve the starter into the water/milk using the fingers, bringing it to a milky consistency, then add to the flour and bring together to a shaggy mass.

Sponge pre-ferment.

Weighing the starter, before incorporating it into the water content of the recipe.

2. Next, slowly, little by little, incorporate the egg yolks.
3. Once incorporated, repeat the process with the butter: it is very important, when working with enriched doughs, that the eggs and butter are gradually introduced so that the fat content does not overwhelm the structure of the dough.
4. When it is all brought together, place the mixture into a lightly oiled bowl, cover and leave overnight in the fridge.

• •

With all the pre-ferments it is advisable, when adding them to the final recipe the following day, to incorporate them into the water content of the recipe and to break them down before adding the rest of the recipe ingredients.

MAKING A SOURDOUGH

There are various techniques that will be of benefit during the sourdough journey.

Direct Sourdough

When baking a direct sourdough (as opposed to making a pre-ferment the day before), the recipe needs to be read the day before. This is because the starter will need to be fed a particular amount, depending on the recipe in question. For example: if the recipe asks for 150g of starter, the starter should be brought out of the fridge, and fed with 75g of rye flour and 75g of water (50/50). After a good stir, the starter can then stay out of the fridge all night, at room temperature, where the extra warmth will make the fermentation process go wild.

The Autolyse Process

The autolyse process is a technique that can be introduced into all bread products, but it is particularly helpful when it comes to making sourdough. It is a more direct use of the starter, instead of making a stiff starter or a pre-ferment. The autolyse process is sometimes referred to as the 'no knead method'. This seems to go against everything bakers are taught: that to build the gluten network needed for the perfect structure, time and pressure must be incorporated in the form of kneading the dough over a period of six to eight minutes. Yes, kneading does speed up the process, and it does help with volume, texture and flavour, however, it is not actually necessary. The 'no knead method' was hailed as a new way of baking in the 1999 cookbook *No Need To Knead*, written by Suzanne Dunaway.

However, in bread-making, nothing is new; it is merely rediscovered. An earlier example of a book with very similar content is Ann Pillsbury's *Bake, The No Knead Way*, written in 1945, long before Dunaway's.

The very first bakers did not have the scientific knowledge that is available today with regards to how a gluten network is created. Nevertheless, they would have understood that leaving their mixture to sit for a period would help with the structure, texture and flavour of the end result. The autolyse process allows the mixture to be introduced at a slower rate and gives the development a more harmonious amalgamation.

The role of salt in bread-making is to tighten the gluten structure. However, in this method, the gluten network is given time to build first and the salt is added later than usual.

Shaggy mass of dough.

THE AUTOLYSE METHOD

1. Bring all the flours together in a bowl.
2. Measure the water.
3. Weigh the starter required for the recipe.
4. Mix the water and starter into a milky consistency.
5. Add the milky concoction into the flour and gently bring together into a shaggy mass. Cover the bowl with cling film and leave for 30 minutes at room temperature, to allow the gluten network to build.
6. Uncover the bowl and evenly sprinkle the salt over the shaggy mass. Add a spritz of water from a water spray bottle to help the salt to dissolve.
7. Using a dough scraper, fold the dough in the bowl, making sure the salt is evenly distributed. The dough will instantly start to tighten and bind together.

Raisin and fennel no-knead method.

The autolyse method is particularly useful when using wholegrain flours as they contain bran, which has sharp edges. When a dough is kneaded in the traditional way, whether by hand or by mixer, this can actually be detrimental to the formation of a strong gluten structure, literally attacking the strands and shredding them. The end result can be a much denser bake.

KNEADING

Wheat flour contains two proteins – gliadin and glutenin – which combine to form gluten. When bread dough is first mixed together, the proteins are mangled and knotted in no particular order. As the dough is kneaded, the proteins line up to form giant chains of amino acids, creating a matrix within the dough itself. It

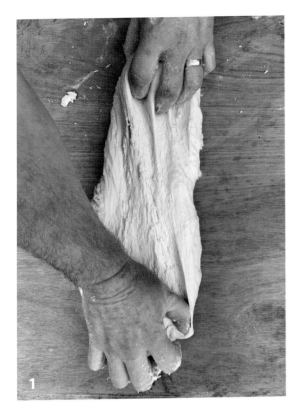

is this matrix that allows the dough to trap gas released by the yeast or other leavening agents, resulting in the rise.

Kneading dough can be a good workout, or you can enlist your trusty mixer to do it for you. Either way, kneading is a science and the tactics involved are specific if you are to achieve a delectable crust and crumb.

This process is all about time and pressure, whether it is being done in a stand mixer or by hand. The autolyse method can be adopted for ease, but hand kneading speeds up the process and also helps a baker to really connect with the dough. Bakers learn through their hands; the feeling of textures changing as the gluten develops and binds together builds knowledge. A good baker becomes a multisensory learner, and this knowledge can then be translated to a stand mixer, if desired.

Different kneading techniques are required depending on the hydration levels of the recipe. For example, the technique for an English loaf with 60% hydration and for a ciabatta with 90–100% hydration will be different. Despite the differences, however, it is still all about time and pressure.

The English Technique

This method is used predominantly for recipes of around 60–70% hydration. It involves a stretch, pull, push action.

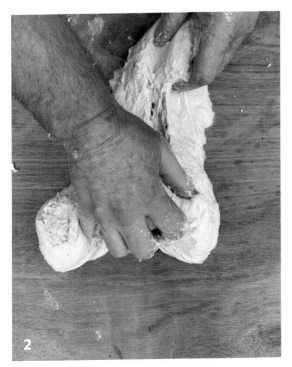

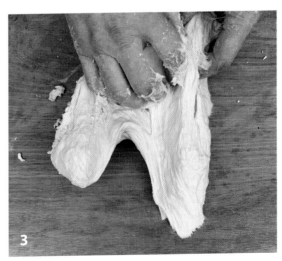

The stretch and fold technique in action.

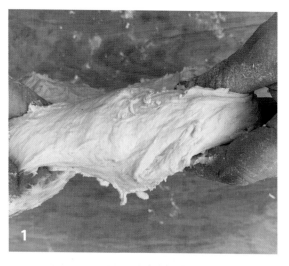
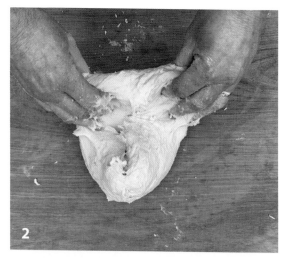
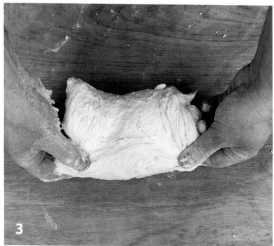

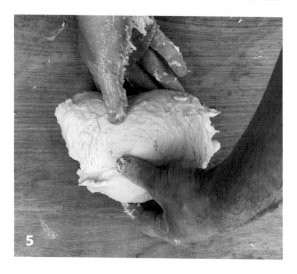

The slap and fold technique in action.

German Technique

This method elongates the dough, lifting it and slapping it on to the table with one hand, not letting go of it, so it is stretched out then folded over. This process is then repeated. This helps to stretch the dough and build the gluten network. The German technique is used mainly for hydration levels of 75–85%.

The Slap, Fold and Turn Technique

Like the German technique, this can also be used for high-hydration doughs. The dough is held with both hands at the top, while the bottom of the dough is slapped on to the table, without letting go. It is folded over top to bottom, and the hands are moved from left to right of the dough, then changing direction with a quarter-turn, whilst repeating the above method in a fluid motion.

Slapping the Dough

This technique is excellent for ciabatta and focaccia, which are both doughs of high hydration. It involves a 'slap and gather': using two hands to scoop up the dough with fingers lifting into the air and then dramatically slapping the dough back on to the work surface and gathering back up between fingers, lifting in to the air, then slapping back down again. This method is not for the faint-hearted and can cause a fair amount of splatter.

DIVIDE AND SHAPE

The final shaping of the sourdough is all about practice, practice and more practice. The baker needs to be able to handle both the dough and the dough scraper simultaneously. Any relocating of dough on the work surface is now the job of the dough scraper, as it can move dough around with ease without ruining the overall shape. It can slide under the dough at speed and is a great help in shaping the dough. The dough scraper is also a great cutting tool to help with the division and transportation of dough to weighing scales.

Shaping the dough is crucial before it goes into a final prove, and expertise at this stage will be the deciding factor in how aesthetically pleasing the finished bread will be. However, this skill cannot be learned overnight. One way to hone hand moulding and shaping skills is to use 'dead' dough – a dough without yeast that can be re-shaped time and time again. It is all about pulling the structure together, in order to identify the weakest part of the dough. If it is not discovered at this point, it will be found by the oven spring, and the bread will burst open.

The Roll

At first glance, this technique resembles a magic trick, but it is all about the hand finding the dimensions of the dough and holding it nice and snug. First, prepare a flour-free surface, as dough needs to gain purchase on the table. Now apply pressure by pushing the dough on to the surface and simultaneously rotating the hands. This will rotate the weak element of the dough to the bottom; this element is known as the 'seam'.

The technique may not come naturally, and some bakers will pick it up more quickly than others. Most people seem to master it eventually, but with one hand only, as opposed to having one piece of dough in each hand.

The Boule

Depending on how big your hands are, a boule can be created by using a pressure and rotation technique, as with the roll. However, it might be easier to use the centre fold method. If the dough is sticky to the touch, add a light dusting of flour to the work surface, then lift out the dough on to the surface with the aid of a dough scraper. Now bring all the edges into the centre, pulling the dough nice and tight, and then remove any excess flour from the table and flip the dough over. Approach the dough with both hands in a V shape at the base of the dough, and rotate until dough is nicely tight and round, with the seam at the bottom.

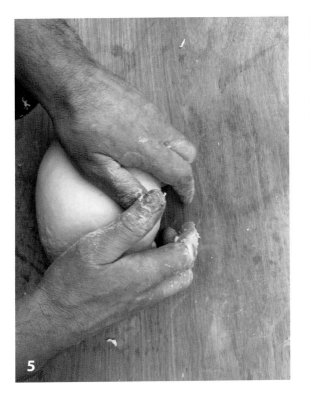

Boule balling technique and the desired end product. When shaping and moulding, ensure you shape your dough into a tight sphere in order to maximize carbon dioxide retention.

Bâtard technique and floured basket.

The Bâtard

To shape the bâtard, turn the dough out on to a lightly floured surface, and gently push out the build-up of gas from the yeast. Now bring the top part of the dough into the centre, then the sides, and then bring the bottom into the centre too. Next, roll the dough over and begin to roll it out slightly, keeping it nice and tight, still leaving a seam on the bottom.

Folding the seams into the centre.

Bâtard technique, step-by-step.

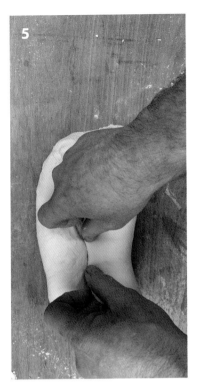
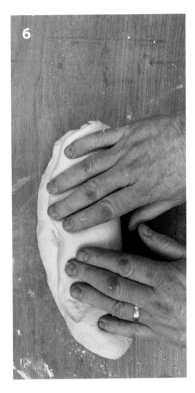

Bâtard technique, step-by-step *(continued)*.

The Baguette

This technique is similar to that used to create the bâtard. When the folds have been made and rolled over the dough, with both hands begin to roll it out with a little pressure. Whilst extending the dough, make sure you keep a track of where the seam is. Remember that the seam is the weak part of the dough; if it is forgotten, the oven will expose it.

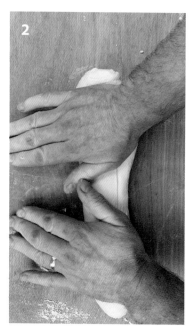

Baguette technique, step-by-step, following on from the bâtard, finishing with the baguette resting in a couche cloth.

The Fougasse

This adorable creature is a French classic, which allows the baker to use some design flair. Turn out the dough on to a lightly floured surface and gently pat out the gas. With the heel of the hand, start to shape the bottom corners, making the dough wider at the bottom. Pull up the top to resemble a triangle, and then use the curved edge of a scraper (or a pizza cutter) and make a cut in the centre, ensuring it does not go all the way through to the top or bottom. Make three cuts on either side of the central cut. Making sure you do not cut into the central cut, and ensuring you do not cut right to the edge, gently tease the three cuts on each side open. This should create the classic leaf shape.

Shaping the fougasse, step-by-step.

Finished fougasse in its classic leaf shape.

PROVING, BULK FERMENTATION AND FOLDING

Proving is a period of fermentation during which bread dough rises to its final shape through a process called respiration. This occurs when yeast feeds on sugar and releases carbon dioxide as a result, distributing air bubbles throughout the dough that cause it to rise. The food for the yeast develops when the starches in flour interact with water and release simple sugars, such as sucrose and glucose.

As the sugar is consumed, the yeast also creates alcohol, which results in the warm, toasty flavours associated with bread. As a rule, the more fermentation the dough undergoes, the better and more complex the bread's flavour will be.

The proving process is extremely time-consuming and demands great patience. The entire fermentation cycle takes place in a number of rounds of rest, referred to as 'first prove' (or 'bulk fermentation'), folding and a 'second prove', and 'final prove' (or 'shaped prove').

First Prove or Bulk Fermentation

This crucial step is key to the bread-making operation and is particularly important when multiple loaves of bread are being made out of one batch of dough. Bulk fermentation occurs when the baker allows the dough to ferment as one larger mass, developing a consistent flavour and rise, before being split and shaped into individual loaves. This is the period when the majority of fermentation takes place and the dough develops much of its taste and texture.

The process will generally take one and a half to two and a half hours at room temperature. The time will depend on the exact temperatures of the dough (warmer dough rises faster than colder dough) and the environment, as well as the ingredient quantities in the dough.

Folding

After bulk fermentation takes place, dough should always be folded, no matter whether you are making one loaf or 100 loaves. Folding the dough, stretching and re-layering it, encourages the gluten structure to develop, which increases the ability of the bread to retain air and moisture.

To fold the bread properly, wet your hands and a spatula with water and scrape the dough from the side of the bowl, manoeuvring it carefully so as not to leave too much dough behind on the sides. Then, gently tug one side of the dough upwards and over in a folding motion, repeating once on each side and allowing the dough to stretch, to redistribute the yeast. For the best end result, this process should be done twice, with half an hour of covered rest between folding.

Bulk fermentation is vital to the success of sourdough bread and this technique builds the structure, giving the strength needed for the perfect sourdough. Bulk fermentation can be the process to which some people completing sourdoughs at home pay the least attention. However, leaving it out will result in an unmanageable spreading of the dough, and a lack of strength and volume.

The Bulk Ferment Method

Most sourdough recipes are of a high hydration, making the dough hard to handle. It may be advisable to add a little oil to the work surface. A little gelatine dissolved in water can also make high-hydration doughs easier to handle. The added benefit to using gelatine is that it results in a better and darker crust. When the dough is turned out, the oil or water/gelatine mixture will provide the barrier needed to handle the operation of the folds.

Repeat the process three more times, giving a 30-minute rest period per fold. The difference in the strength of the dough will be notable every time the process is repeated.

Do not get this confused with the final prove; this process is all about building the strength and the flavour profile.

Final Prove

When it come to the final prove, the dough will need to be supported during the process. This can be in the form of a loaf tin, banneton basket or a couche cloth. If using a loaf tin, grease it or line it with parchment. Silicone paper is the paper of choice for all

Sourdough in a basket during its final prove.

professionals. The couche cloth or basket will need a liberal dusting of flour as opposed to greasing.

When it comes to a loaf, the shaping is the same as with the bâtard, making sure the seam is on the bottom of the tin. Conversely, when using the banneton basket or the couche cloth, the seam will be facing up. Remember, once the prove has been achieved, the products will be tipped out of the basket and the dough will be the right way up!

• •

BASIC SOURDOUGH

Ingredients

Starter	195g
Water	315g
Strong white bread flour	480g
Wheat bran	10g
Fine sea salt	12g

Now the starter is over six days old, vibrant and active. The day before starting to bake the sourdough, check the recipe and feed the starter according to the percentages of flour and water needed. As a final check, pop a spoonful of the starter into a cup of warm water. If it floats, it is good; if it sinks, the starter needs a little time to warm up (but do not let it get too warm). Once the correct amount of starter has been measured out for the recipe, it can go back into the fridge.

Get everything you need in the same location – preparation is everything:

- Dough scraper
- Olive oil; this may be a little sticky
- Dusting flour
- Water spray
- Banneton basket
- Good sharp blade

Method

1. Take your starter and add the water to it, combining into a milky substance, then combine your salt, flour and wheat bran into a second bowl.

2. Add the flour mix to the first bowl and mix using one hand until a dough is formed. (Keep the other hand clean for using utensils, and so on.) This will take only a couple of minutes. Use a plastic dough scraper around the bowl to make sure all the flour is incorporated.

3. Now turn out on to a clean dry surface – any surface is fine as long as it is clean. Knead the dough for around eight minutes then shape with the aid of the scraper into something that resembles a smooth ball. Lift it back into the bowl with the smooth side up. Cover the bowl with a shower cap – much less fiddly than cling film or a damp tea towel – and leave it to rest at room temperature for around an hour.

4. After this time, give the dough a fold in the bowl, using slightly wet hands to prevent it sticking. Pull a section of the dough out to the side and fold it into the middle of the ball. Repeat this going around the ball of dough until you get back to the beginning (four or five folds). Use the scraper to turn the dough upside down, then cover the bowl and leave for another 5–10 minutes.

5. Repeat this three times. After the final fold, cover the bowl again and leave to rest for one hour at room temperature.

6. Turn the dough out of the bowl on to a lightly floured surface. Stretch out one side of the dough and fold it into the middle. Repeat this with each of the four 'sides' of the dough. Put the dough back in the bowl upside down and leave to rest for another hour at room temperature.

7. To shape a round loaf, once the dough has rested, turn it out on to a lightly floured surface. Stretch one side of the dough out and fold it into the middle. Repeat this all around the outside of the dough until you get back to your starting point. Flip it so the seam side is facing down. Use your left hand to hold the dough in place and use your right hand to rotate the dough, tucking it under and tightening it as you go around. (If you are left-handed, you might want to use your right hand to stabilize and your left hand to rotate.) The idea here

is to increase the strength of the dough without tearing it. The final surface of the dough should feel taut to the touch.

8. Place the dough seam side up into a floured proving basket, and then into the fridge for an overnight prove.

9. To test whether the dough has proved enough, press your finger about 2–3cm into it, then remove. If the dough pushes back out slowly, it is ready. If it springs back quickly, the dough is under-proved; if it does not spring back at all, it is over-proved. If the dough is over-proved, you need to de-gas it, re-shape and prove again. Remember, the second attempt will take half the time to achieve the full prove.

10. Preheat the oven to 250°C/fan 240°C/gas mark 10, or the highest temperature on your model. Place a roasting dish in the bottom of the oven to heat up, and a flat baking tray on one of the shelves. Fill a cup with water and place to one side ready to use.

11. When the oven is up to temperature, take the hot baking tray out, lightly dust it with flour and then turn the dough from the proving basket out on to it. Slash the dough with a sharp knife, using one quick, smooth action, to give a nice clean line; do not 'saw' at it. In the bakery, we use a single diagonal slash down the loaf, but there are endless variations. This is an opportunity to be creative and come up with your own distinctive pattern, as bakers would have done in the very early days of baking, when they were using communal village ovens.

12. Place the baking tray in the oven and pour the cup of water into the preheated roasting dish at the bottom. The moisture created will make the dough lighter, help to set the crust and give it a lovely sheen.

13. Turn the temperature down to 240°C/fan 220°C/gas mark 9, and bake for 30–35 minutes.

14. To check if the bread is baked through, tap the bottom – it should sound hollow.

15. Leave the bread to cool for at least an hour before eating.

• •

Incorporating salt and water into the starter.

TIMES AND TEMPERATURES, AND STEAM

Follow the baking times and temperatures according to the type and size of your product, but always try to add steam to the oven too, to give that extra crispy crust. This can be done in a number of ways: use a spray bottle to spray water on to the base and sides of the oven as soon as the dough has been loaded; place a tray on the base of the oven, put the product in and then drop a handful of ice cubes into the tray; or place a tray on the base of the oven and pour water into the tray at the same stage.

The steam will give the crust a nice shiny golden colour that crisps and cracks when exiting the oven during the temperature change; bread that has not had a hit of steam can look quite dull. The steam helps to keep the crust soft during the first five minutes in the oven, whilst also encouraging the natural sugars in the flour to caramelize, thus developing the colour. It also helps to keep the oven spring more even. The Dutch cast-iron oven is particularly effective in this respect, as it has a lid, which helps to retain the moisture in the dough and creates its own steamy environment.

The following time and temperature guide will give a good indicator when it comes to proving your bread.

SCORING TECHNIQUES

The dough is scored after its prove and just before it is loaded into the oven. The reason for scoring bread is simple: once the dough hits the heat from the oven, it starts to expand – bakers call this the oven spring. Scoring the dough allows the baker to create a weak spot in the loaf, thereby controlling the split caused by the oven spring. If it is not scored, the heat will find a weak spot in the structure of the bread, and that will become the seam of the dough – not necessarily in the right place.

Different bread products are scored in different ways, but the main aim is that the cuts should be symmetrical, and of a consistent depth of 6mm (about a quarter of an inch).

Proving times with differing outcomes

Time	Temperature	Outcome
24hrs	2°C/36°F	Flavour enhanced but a reduction in volume
12–16hrs	4°C/39°F	Flavour enhanced and good volume
14hrs	13°C/55°F	Less sour and good volume

Baking times and temperatures

Product	Weight	Oven	Water injection time	Preheat temp.	Baking temp.	Lid on	Lid off	Total bake time
Sourdough boule	1kg	Dutch cast-iron	n/a	250°C/482°F	230°C/446°F	40 mins	For last 15 mins	55 mins
Sourdough boule	500g	Dutch cast-iron	n/a	250°C/482°F	230°C/446°F	30 mins	For last 10 mins	40 mins
Sourdough roll	80g	Baking stone	Spritz, water bottle	250°C/482°F	220°C/428°F	n/a	n/a	20–25 mins

Scoring dough is all about confidence. Practising on 'dead' dough is a good way of honing skills and building that confidence. It is also useful when testing out a new design. Your design can be based on a stencil that you make yourself or buy online, or you can make a template from natural products such as leaves, which of course come in many different shapes and sizes.

There are specialist pieces of equipment available for scoring, but a simple razor blade or craft knife will work well, as they are flexible and sharp (and cheap!). You can make your own baker's lame, but if you are not confident of being able to do this, there are many artisan bread websites where you can acquire one.

Begin with a simple but effective cut, inserting just the tip of the blade into the dough. Cut in one fluid motion. The movement should not be sawing back and forth like slicing a baked loaf, but nice and confident and at a constant depth.

The best way to demonstrate the scoring techniques is visually. The following images will give you a useful set of go-to designs, but as you practise, practise, practise, and build your confidence, you will be able to make your own works of art.

Classic sourdough with slashes cut through the top in order to take control of the impact of the oven spring.

Square score.

Central score.

Vertical score.

Diamond score.

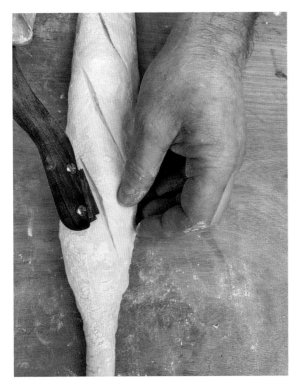

Scoring a baguette.

Herringbone score.

CHAPTER 4

CREATIVE SOURDOUGH

Taste is a personal matter. The element you want to be most pronounced in your bread will vary depending on who is eating it, what it is being paired with, the occasion, and so on. Taste panels of friends and customers can really assist in determining this. The same questions come up in every sourdough class I teach: some people will ask why their sourdough is not sour enough, and others will ask how they can make theirs less sour. If you make the decision as to which camp you want to be in at an early stage, then it is possible to adapt your starter to suit your preferences. This is done by altering the usual 50/50 proportions of

flour to water: for example, having more liquid in the starter (for example, 50g flour and 60g water) will cause the bread to taste more sour. Conversely, if the starter is too liquid, and the end result too sour, the ingredients can be changed to 60g flour and 40g water. These

Dough with thyme inclusion whilst kneading.

Close-up of sprouting grains inclusion.

Creative sourdough, demonstrating natural colourings, blue pea and pumpkin, topped with teff and quinoa seeds.

SPROUTED GRAINS

Close-up during the sprouting process.

Kilner jars full of freshly sprouted grains.

Sprouted grains, which have just begun their germination process, will give the bread a completely different texture. They are considered by some to be an extremely healthy option and their use is becoming more popular. You can sprout your own grains, but always check the source. Use organic; non-organic grains have usually been treated with a fungicide or heat treatment, and will be less likely to germinate. When it comes to grain choice, again, you can play around until you find the perfect flavour combination.

Close-up of colourful sprouted grains.

Method

1. Empty the grains into a clean plastic container and pour in filtered water, making sure the grains are covered. (This process takes a while, so do a larger batch than you need; once they have germinated, pop the excess into the freezer for future bakes.)
2. Soak the grains overnight at room temperature.
3. Drain away the water, return the grains to the container and place a paper towel over them, then fit the container lid and leave at room temperature overnight.
4. Rinse the grains in cool water, return to a clean container, cover with fresh filtered water if the grains feel dry, and reapply the paper towel.
5. Repeat steps 3 and 4 and leave overnight until the grains have sprouted.

proportions are not set in stone, and it is perfectly feasible to play around with them until the desired level of sourness is achieved.

INCLUSIONS

Inclusions are a way of packing a sourdough with added flavour, texture and nutrients, using spices, herbs, nuts, seeds, fruits, cheeses – whatever is desired. Favourite flavour combinations that complement each other on a plate can be transferred to the bread mixture, where they are likely to achieve the same effect. As a rule, any powdered spices (such as cinnamon) can go into the bread mixture right at the beginning alongside the flour. This helps to give the dough a nice even colour; if the spices are added to the completed dough, it is more difficult to mix them in thoroughly and there is likely to be a marbling effect. On the other hand, inclusions such as seeds, nuts, fruits, cheeses and herbs should be added only after the gluten structure has been built. Knead the dough and leave it to rest for 30 minutes before mixing them in.

Sourdough with cherries to exaggerate the sour tang.

Inclusion options for added texture and flavour.

Creative sourdough with figs and goats' cheese.

Inclusions should always be added with a gentle approach, to ensure that they are evenly distributed. Going in too heavy with something such as fruit will cause it to split, which will in turn cause a bleed into the dough. This will discolour the dough and release all the sugars from the fruit into it, thus slowing down the proving time. Nuts should be broken down into manageable pieces before being added to the dough.

In my classes in London, I always use the walnut and stilton sourdough to demonstrate how to add inclusions. It is a lovely combination of flavours, and an ideal staple for the Christmas cheese board. The stilton should be broken into one-inch pieces and kept reasonably intact when being distributed into the dough; when the bread has been baked, the crumb should be studded with melted jewels of stilton rather than homogenized.

Inclusions are a great way of making many different products from a large dough mixture: just divide and include.

Fig and goats' cheese focaccia.

WALNUT AND STILTON/ SPRING ONION AND BRIE

Using the basic sourdough recipe from Chapter 3, this will achieve two good-sized boules with different inclusions in each.

Ingredients

Ingredients	
Water	315g
Starter	195g
Strong white bread flour	480g
Wheat bran	10g
Fine sea salt	6g
Spring onions	4 (3 for inside, 1 large for decoration)
Brie	Approx. 200g
Stilton	A quantity according to personal taste
Walnuts, broken up	50g

Remember: The starter will need to be fed the night before, with 100g of rye flour and 100g of water, and left out of the fridge all night. Just before using it, drop a tiny amount in a bowl of warm water; if it floats, it is ready to go.

Method

1. Combine the water needed with the starter necessary for the recipe until it resembles a milky consistency.
2. Combine the flour, wheat bran and salt and then add the dry ingredients to the first bowl and mix using one hand until a dough forms. This will take only a couple of minutes. (If you use only one hand, you can keep the other one clean for using utensils, and so on.) Use a plastic dough scraper around the bowl to make sure all the flour is mixed in.
3. Empty the dough on to the counter and knead for around 8 minutes, or use a stand mixer with a dough hook attachment. Once the dough has been kneaded successfully, use the scraper to shape it into a smooth ball and pop this into the bowl smooth side up. Cover the bowl with a shower cap or damp tea towel and leave it to rest at room temperature.

Walnut and stilton sourdough, with a leaf used as a stencil.

Spring onion and brie sourdough.

4. After 5–10 minutes, give the dough a fold in the bowl, using slightly wet hands to prevent it sticking. Pull a section of the dough out to the side and fold it into the middle of the ball. Repeat this, going around the ball of dough until you get back to the beginning (four or five folds). Use the scraper to turn the dough upside down, cover the bowl and leave for another 5–10 minutes.

5. Split the dough in half and add the spring onions and brie to one piece and the stilton and walnut pieces to the other. Adding the inclusions, 50g of each, will give the dough an added weight of 100g. Aim for a gentle and even distribution.

6. Repeat the folding method three times. After the final fold, cover the bowl again and leave to rest for one hour at room temperature.

7. Turn the dough out of the bowl on to a lightly floured surface. Stretch out one side of the dough and fold it into the middle. Repeat this with each of the four 'sides' of the dough. Put the dough back in the bowl upside down and leave to rest for another hour at room temperature.

8. To shape a round loaf, once the dough has rested, turn it out on to a lightly floured surface. Stretch one side of the dough out and fold it into the middle. Repeat this all around the outside of the dough until you get back to your starting point. Flip it so the seam side is facing down. Use your left hand to hold the dough in place and your right hand to rotate the dough, tucking it under and tightening it as you go around. (If you are left-handed, you might want to use your right hand to stabilize and your left hand to rotate.) The idea here is to increase the strength of the dough without tearing it. The final surface of the dough should feel taut to the touch.

9. Dust the proving baskets with flour. Split a large spring onion and place it at the bottom of one basket, then shape the spring onion and brie dough and place it into the basket, with the seam facing up. Place a handful of walnuts in the bottom of the other basket, and put in the walnut and stilton dough. Put the baskets into the fridge for an overnight prove.

10. To test whether the dough has proved enough, press your finger about 2–3cm into it, then remove. If the dough pushes back out slowly, it is ready. If it springs back quickly, the dough is under-proved; if it does not spring back at all, it is over-proved. Re-shape it and leave out at room temperature until it is at optimum prove.

11. Preheat the oven to 250°C/fan 240°C/gas mark 10, or the highest temperature on your model. Place a roasting dish in the bottom of the oven to heat up, and a flat baking tray on one of the shelves. Fill a cup with water and place to one side ready to use.

12. When the oven is up to temperature, take the hot baking tray out, lightly dust it with flour and then turn the dough from the proving basket out on to the tray. Slash the dough with a sharp knife, using one quick, smooth action to give a clean line; do not 'saw' at the dough. In the bakery, we use a single diagonal slash down the loaf, but there are endless variations; this is an opportunity to be creative and come up with your own distinctive pattern.

13. Place the baking tray in the oven and pour the cup of water into the preheated roasting dish at the bottom. The moisture created will make the dough lighter, help to set the crust and give it a lovely sheen.

14. Turn the temperature down to 240°C/fan 220°C/gas mark 9 and bake for 30–35 minutes. To check if the bread is baked through, tap the bottom – it should sound hollow.

15. Leave the bread to cool for at least an hour before eating.

• •

BAKING WITH RYE FLOUR

Rye flour gives a lovely depth of flavour and in Germany and Russia most breads can be found with an element of this ingredient within their structure. Many classic French breads also tend to include a certain percentage of rye. Rye flour is low in protein, at around 6%, so a high percentage of rye in a bread recipe will result in a denser crumb. A great flavour combination to accompany 100% rye is raisin and caraway.

RAISIN AND CARAWAY RYE SOURDOUGH

Remember: The starter will need feeding the night before.

Day 1: Pre-ferment ingredients

Rye flour	100g
Cold water	140g
Starter	75g

Method: Day 1

Add the starter into the water and mix into a milky consistency, add to flour and fold, resulting in a wet mass. Cover and leave out overnight at room temperature.

Day 2 ingredients

Honey	8g
Tepid water	100g
Rye flour	150g
Fine sea salt	5g
Caraway seeds	8g
Raisins	80g

Method: Day 2

1. Place honey into the water and give this a good stir.
2. Place all the ingredients into the pre-ferment and add the water and honey mix. With a scraper bring the mixture together, making sure everything is evenly distributed.
3. Give the work surface a good dusting of rye flour and line a 1lb loaf tin.
4. Turn the dough out on to the floured surface and roll back and forth – this mixture is incredibly sticky, but remember, 6% protein, 100% rye is all about bringing together, not kneading!
5. Roll the dough over and lift into the tin, then give the top a good dusting of rye flour. Cover and prove at room temperature for around two hours, until there is a volume of 10mm above the tin.
6. Preheat oven to 240°C/fan 230°/gas mark 8. Give the oven a good spritz of water whilst the loaf is in the oven and bake for 40–45 minutes. The aim here is a nice dark bake.
7. After baking, remove the loaf from the tin and leave to cool thoroughly (for 24 hours). A long cooling period is recommended when baking 100% rye because of the density.

Experiment with styles and structures, such as this classic couronne.

MORE FLAVOUR, COLOUR AND TEXTURE

Adding Colour

With a little creativity, a simple sourdough can be turned into a real show-stopper, for example, by adding a little colour to the dough with a pinch of turmeric or purple sweet potato.

Sourdoughs coloured with natural spices.

The appearance of the sourdough can be enhanced using toppings and inclusions.

Wild garlic sourdough rolls with fresh flours, during their final prove.

Wild Garlic

Wild garlic is abundant in most woodlands, so is freely available with a little foraging. The faint garlic taste combines well with sourness in this sourdough. Wild garlic also lends itself to creative designs – after using the green leaves of the plant in the recipe, set aside the beautiful white flower head to stick in the top of each roll.

Freshly baked wild garlic rolls.

WILD GARLIC SOURDOUGH ROLLS

Use a stiff starter for this one, to ensure the sour flavour does not overpower the delicate flavour of the wild garlic.

Day 1: Stiff starter ingredients	
Strong white bread flour	100g
Water	50g
Starter	50g

Method: Day 1

1. Mix your starter into the water and merge together into a milky consistency. Add this to the flour and work this into a ball.
2. Cover and leave out overnight.

Day 2 ingredients	
Strong white bread flour	455g
Rye flour	30g
Fine sea salt	9g
Water	315g
Chopped wild garlic	150g
Polenta or semolina	15g

Method: Day 2

1. Mix the dry ingredients in a second bowl and add to the first bowl, then mix with the water using one hand until a dough is formed. (Keep the other hand clean for using utensils, and so on.) This will take only a couple of minutes. Use a plastic dough scraper around the bowl to make sure all the flour is mixed in.
2. Cover the bowl with a shower cap or damp tea towel and leave it to rest at room temperature.
3. After 5–10 minutes, give the dough a fold in the bowl, using slightly wet hands to prevent it sticking. Pull a section of the dough out to the side and fold it into the middle of the ball. Repeat this going around the ball of dough until you get back to the beginning (four or five folds). Use the scraper to turn the dough upside down, cover the bowl and leave for another 5–10 minutes.
4. Repeat these folds a further three times. After the final fold, cover the bowl again and leave to rest for one hour at room temperature.
5. Turn the dough out of the bowl on to a lightly floured surface. Stretch out one side of the dough and fold it into the middle. Repeat this with each of the four 'sides' of the dough. Put the dough back in the bowl upside down and leave to rest for another hour at room temperature.
6. Now, add the chopped wild garlic and fold into the dough, distributing it evenly. Stretch one side of the dough out and fold it into the middle. Repeat this all around the outside of the dough until you get back to your starting point. Flip it so that the seam side is facing down. Use your left hand to hold the dough in place and your right hand to rotate the dough, tucking it under and tightening it as you go around. (If you are left-handed, you might want to use your right hand to stabilize and your left hand to rotate.) The idea here is to increase the strength of the dough without tearing it. The final surface of the dough should feel quite taut to the touch.
7. Divide and shape: weigh these into 120g pieces, hand-mould into shape, and bring out the white garlic flowers that were set aside. Snip the top of the dough and insert the flowers, then lightly dust a tea towel with polenta or semolina and slide on to a baking tray. Place rolls on to the tray, then into the fridge for an overnight prove.
8. To test whether the dough has proved enough, press your finger about 2–3cm into it, then remove. If the dough pushes back out slowly, it is ready. If it springs back quickly, the dough is under-proved; if it does not spring back at all, it is over-proved. Re-shape it and leave out at room temperature until it is at optimum prove.
9. Preheat the oven to 230°C/fan 220°C/gas mark 9. Place a roasting dish in the bottom of the oven to heat up, and a flat baking tray on one of the shelves. Fill a cup with water and place to one side ready to use.

10. When the oven is up to temperature, transfer the rolls on to the baking tray. Place the tray in the oven and pour the cup of water into the preheated roasting dish at the bottom. The moisture created will make the dough lighter, help to set the crust and give it a lovely sheen.

11. Turn the temperature down to 220°C/fan 210°C/gas mark 9 and bake for 30–35 minutes. To check if the bread rolls are baked through, tap the bottom – they should sound hollow.

12. Leave the bread to cool for at least an hour before eating.

ANCIENT GRAINS

The 'ancient grains' are the very first grains that were cultivated by our forefathers. They are high in fibre, vitamin B, potassium, magnesium and antioxidants, and have recently been the subject of a revival, spurred on by the same sort of health-conscious and foodie-minded people who started the Artisan Movement. The flour produced from ancient grains is low in protein, and therefore low in gluten. Some say that, if we had stuck with these grains, the prevalence of gluten intolerance today would be much lower.

Grains during the milling process.

Low-protein flours result in a dense loaf, which perhaps explains why the use of ancient grains had diminished. While some people really like the dense structure, others prefer a little 'bounce' to their bread. However, the health benefits are evident and, when these flours are combined into sourdough, they create excellent flavour, with nutty undertones.

Basic Ancient Grain Sourdough

There are a couple of methods here: either make a different flour combination that still gives the gluten needed, or add vital gluten powder to ancient flours, to give the strength needed to give a good strong gluten network. This will provide a loaf that is full of flavour, as well as bounce and volume.

· ·

ANCIENT GRAIN SOURDOUGH

Either use a poolish or a stiff starter, or go for a direct mix. Repeat the process of feeding the starter the night before and leaving it out of the fridge. Just before using it, drop a little into a cup of warm water and ensure that it floats.

Ingredients	
Starter	150g
Water	280g
Strong white bread flour	340g
Einkorn flour	55g
Emmer flour	55g
Spelt flour	50g
Salt	10g
Malt powder	1g
Sprouted grains	100g

Method

1. Mix the starter and water together into a milky liquid. In a second bowl, use one hand to combine all the ingredients, apart from the sprouted grains, until a dough starts to form. (Leave the other hand clean for using utensils, and so on.) This takes only a couple of minutes. Use a plastic dough scraper around the bowl to make sure all the flour is mixed in. Cover the bowl with a shower cap or damp tea towel and leave it to rest at room temperature.

2. After 5–10 minutes, give the dough a fold in the bowl, using slightly wet hands to prevent it sticking. Pull a section of the dough out to the side and fold it into the middle of the ball. Repeat this going around the ball of dough until you get back to the beginning (four or five folds). Use the scraper to turn the dough upside down, cover the bowl and leave for another 5–10 minutes.

3. Repeat these folds a further three times. After the final fold, cover the bowl again and leave to rest for one hour at room temperature.

4. Turn the dough out of the bowl on to a lightly floured surface. Stretch out one side of the dough and fold it into the middle. Repeat this with each of the four 'sides' of the dough.

5. Put the dough back in the bowl upside down and leave to rest for another hour at room temperature, then add the sprouted grains and distribute evenly.

6. To shape a round loaf, once the dough has rested, turn it out on to a lightly floured surface. Stretch one side of the dough out and fold it into the middle. Repeat this all around the outside of the dough until you get back to your starting point. Flip it so that the seam side is facing down. Use your left hand to hold the dough in place and your right hand to rotate the dough, tucking it under and tightening it as you go around. (If you are left-handed, you might want to use your right hand to stabilize and your left hand to rotate.) The idea here is to increase the strength of the dough without tearing it. The final surface of the dough should feel taut to the touch.

7. Place the dough seam side up into a floured proving basket, and then into the fridge for an overnight prove.

8. To test whether the dough has proved enough, press your finger about 2–3cm into it, then remove. If the dough pushes back out slowly, it is ready. If it springs back quickly, the dough is under-proved;

if it does not spring back at all, it is over-proved. Re-shape it and leave out at room temperature until it is at optimum prove.

9. Preheat the oven to 250°C/fan 240°C/gas mark 10 or the highest temperature on your model. Place a roasting dish in the bottom of the oven to heat up, and a flat baking tray on one of the shelves. Fill a cup with water and place to one side ready to use.

10. When the oven is up to temperature, take the hot baking tray out, lightly dust it with flour and then turn the dough from the proving basket out on to the tray. Slash the dough with a sharp knife, using one quick, smooth action, to give a nice clean line; do not 'saw' at it. In the bakery, we use a single diagonal slash down the loaf, but there are endless variations; this is an opportunity to be creative and come up with your own distinctive pattern.

11. Place the baking tray in the oven and pour the cup of water into the preheated roasting dish at the bottom. The moisture created will make the dough lighter, help to set the crust and give it a lovely sheen.

12. Turn the temperature down to 240°C/fan 220°C/gas mark 9 and bake for 30–35 minutes. To check if the bread is baked through, tap the bottom – it should sound hollow.

13. Leave the bread to cool for at least an hour before eating.

● ●

Spelt and Buckwheat

It is worth setting aside a little experimental time to have a play with ancient flour and seed combinations. One great flavoursome loaf I come back to time after time combines spelt, buckwheat and honey. It is a delicious marriage of ancient flours and seeds from around the world. Spelt was a staple around central Europe and northern Spain and has been used by bakers since the Bronze Age, while buckwheat is a favourite from south-east Asia. The seeds are amaranth, a favourite of the Aztecs, and teff, from Ethiopia.

● ●

SPELT, BUCKWHEAT AND HONEY SOURDOUGH

This is a large bread, so it should be proved in a large banneton basket and baked in a Dutch oven.

Day 1: Starter feed ingredients	
Rye flour	75g
Water	75g
Starter	50g

Method: Day 1

Mix 75g of rye flour and 75g water giving you the 150g required. Add and mix in with the main starter and leave loosely covered at room temperature overnight.

Day 2 ingredients	
Spelt flour	400g
Buckwheat flour	100g
Fine sea salt	8g
Starter	150g
Water	310g
Amaranth seeds	30g
Teff seeds	30g
Olive oil	10g
Caster sugar	8g
Honey	40g

Method: Day 2

1. In one bowl, combine the two flours with the salt. In another large bowl, mix together the recipe starter with the water, seeds and other ingredients, and mix gently.

2. Add the flour mix to the second bowl and mix using one hand until a dough begins to form. (Keep the other hand clean for using utensils, and so on.) This will take only a couple of minutes. Use a plastic dough scraper around the bowl to make sure all the flour is mixed in. Cover the bowl with a shower

Spelt, honey and buckwheat sourdough.

cap or damp tea towel and leave it to rest at room temperature.

3. After 5–10 minutes, give the dough a fold in the bowl, using slightly wet hands to prevent it sticking. Pull a section of the dough out to the side and fold it into the middle of the ball. Repeat this going around the ball of dough until you get back to the beginning (four or five folds). Use the scraper to turn the dough upside down, cover the bowl and leave for another 5–10 minutes.

4. Repeat these three times. After the final fold, cover the bowl again and leave to rest for one hour at room temperature.

5. Turn the dough out of the bowl on to a lightly floured surface. Stretch out one side of the dough and fold it into the middle. Repeat this with each of the four 'sides' of the dough.

6. Put the dough back in the bowl upside down and leave to rest for another hour at room temperature.

7. To shape a round loaf, once the dough has rested, turn it out on to a lightly floured surface. Stretch one side of the dough out and fold it into the middle. Repeat this all around the outside of the dough until you get back to your starting point. Flip it so the seam side is facing down. Use your left hand to hold the dough in place and your right hand to rotate the dough, tucking it under and tightening it as you go around. (If you are left-handed, you might want to use your right hand to stabilize and your left hand to rotate.) The idea here is to increase the strength of the dough without tearing it. The final surface of the dough should feel taut to the touch.

8. Place the dough so that the seam is facing up and the seeds facing down in a round proving basket. Give the basket a light dusting of flour: this will prevent the dough from sticking, now into the fridge for an overnight prove.

9. To test whether the dough has proved enough, press your finger about 2–3cm into it, then remove. If the dough pushes back out slowly, it is ready. If it springs back quickly, the dough is under-proved; if it does not spring back at all, it is over-proved. Re-shape it and leave out at room temperature until it is at optimum prove.

10. Preheat the oven to 250°C/fan 240°C/gas mark 10 or the highest temperature on your model. Place a roasting dish in the bottom of the oven to heat up, and a flat baking tray on one of the shelves. Fill a cup with water and place to one side ready to use.

11. When the oven is up to temperature, take the hot baking tray out, lightly dust it with flour and then turn the dough from the proving basket out on to the tray. Slash the dough with a sharp knife, using one quick, smooth action, to give a nice clean line; do not 'saw' at it. In the bakery, we use a single diagonal slash down the loaf, but there are endless variations; this is an opportunity to be creative and come up with your own distinctive pattern.

12. Place the baking tray in the oven and pour the cup of water into the preheated roasting dish at the bottom. The moisture created will make the dough lighter, help to set the crust and give it a lovely sheen.

13. Turn the temperature down to 240°C/fan 220°C/gas mark 9 and bake for 30–35 minutes. To check if the bread is baked through, tap the bottom – it should sound hollow.

14. Leave the bread to cool for at least an hour before eating.

● ●

GLUTEN-FREE PRODUCTS

Gluten is a protein found in several types of grain, including wheat, spelt, rye and barley and, therefore, in most cereals and breads. It comprises gliadin and glutenin, which are effectively the elastic, rubbery elements in grains that bind the dough in bread and other baked goods and help to give a spongy consistency. An intolerance to this protein can cause digestive problems such as gassiness, abdominal pain or diarrhoea.

Gluten intolerance is sometimes confused with coeliac disease, or thought of as a food allergy. While avoiding particular foods is a treatment strategy for all three, the conditions are not the same. Food intolerances involve the digestive

The essential ingredients for a gluten-free bake

system. With a food allergy, the immune system overreacts to a particular food, causing symptoms that are potentially serious or even life-threatening. Coeliac disease is an inherited autoimmune disorder that can damage the small intestine. A food intolerance is an adverse reaction to gluten, resulting in symptoms such as bloating and constipation. These issues are not life-threatening but they can be debilitating.

In some people who suffer from a gluten intolerance, the digestive system seems to be perfectly happy digesting sourdough bread. This makes perfect sense: during the long proving period necessary for sourdough, the gluten is under attack, resulting in lower levels of the protein.

However, a small percentage of people, particularly those who suffer with coeliac disease, rather than having a low-lying intolerance, need to avoid gluten completely. Over the last few years, this has become more widely recognized and there is now a broader range of gluten-free options available both in supermarkets and in restaurants. Just because someone cannot tolerate gluten does not mean that they do not want to experiment in the kitchen, and they will most certainly want to be able to bake their own fresh bread. Sourdough should be experienced and enjoyed by everyone.

Baking with Gluten-Free Flours

I began reading about and experimenting with

Gluten-free starters have a different texture; they should leave a visible trail across the surface.

gluten-free breads to help out a friend, who desperately wanted to try sourdough. Baking with gluten-free flours is rather different from working with other types. For a start, kneading is out of the equation. As a gluten structure is not being built, the raw, uncooked mixture that will later create a gluten-free bread is similar to a cake mixture. The same comparison can be applied to the baking of gluten-free products. With many gluten-free recipes, the oven door should not be opened during the baking process, as this will cause the bread to deflate. Also, the starches in the mixture require the water to be a little warmer, to help the binding process. Naturally, if a sour element is sought in a gluten-free bread, a gluten-free starter will be required. Good candidates for the non-gluten flour in such a starter are brown rice flour, sorghum flour or teff flour, all of which work equally well.

To build a starter, measure out around 50g of your chosen flour, perhaps teff to begin with. This is the point at which the method changes. Slowly add water, starting with 50g, but mix until it has a consistency similar to thick cream, where the spoon leaves a trail on the top.

Once again, leave the mixture out uncovered, save for a tea towel or piece of muslin cloth. Leave it around 12 hours, then check it and feed it again in the same way until it has a smooth creamy consistency. Keep doing this for around six days; by then there should be some tiny bubbles apparent. Once these bubbles are visible and the starter domes – almost as if it is proving – then it is ready to use.

Making gluten-free bread is not all about the flour. The baker also has to think of a substitute for the missing gluten. This can come in the form of xanthan gum, which is a binding agent that helps to provide structure to the bread. However, some people are intolerant to it, in which case you will need to look at eggs or natural starches to act as some kind of binding agent.

Flour and Starch Mixtures

There are a number of good combinations of different flours and starches. The best way is to make a large batch; if you use the ratio of 70% wholegrain flours to 30% starches or white flours, it will be a great time saver. Make up 1000g of wholegrain flour mix.

First, mix together 700g of any combination of the following flours:

Amaranth
Brown rice
Buckwheat
Corn
Millet
Oat
Quinoa
Roasted soy
Sorghum
Sweet brown rice
Teff

For example, you could blend together 100g each of brown rice, buckwheat, millet, quinoa, sorghum, sweet brown rice and teff, or, for a simpler mix, 350g of buckwheat and 350g of millet. Afterwards, throw in 300g of any combination of the following starches:

Arrowroot
Corn starch
Potato starch
Tapioca flour
White rice flour

CHIA AND LINSEED SOURDOUGH LOAF

Day 1: Pre-ferment ingredients	
Tepid water	80g
Starter	80g
White rice flour	50g
Buckwheat flour	50g

Method: Day 1

Mix the water together with the starter, then add to the flour and mix further until all is evenly incorporated. Cover with cling film and leave out at room temperature overnight. The next day it should be bubbling away nicely.

Day 2 ingredients

White rice flour	85g
Buckwheat flour	20g
Salt	4g
Caster sugar	12g
Chia seeds	20g
Linseeds	20g
Tepid water	75g
White wine vinegar	1 tsp
Medium-sized egg	1
Combine separately 10g each of the chia and linseeds and set side for topping	

Method: Day 2

1. Add the flours, salt, caster sugar, seeds (except those set aside for the topping) and a third of the water to the pre-ferment and combine.
2. Make a well in the centre of the mixture and add the white wine vinegar and egg, and the rest of the water. Combine together until the mixture resembles a thick batter. Cover and leave at room temperature for 30 minutes.
3. Line a 1lb loaf tin with baking parchment. Use olive oil to brush the sides of the parchment and dust with the combination of the chia seeds and linseeds.
4. Tip the dough on to a lightly floured surface and pull the sides together making a seam. Place into the loaf tin seam side down, then glaze the top with beaten egg and dust with the seed combination. Cover the loaf and prove until the dough is around half an inch above the tin.
5. Preheat the oven to 180°C/gas mark 4 and bake for 40 minutes, remembering not to open the oven door.

SOURDOUGH GLUTEN-FREE FOCACCIA

Day 1: Poolish ingredients

Your choice of flour and starch combination	50g
Water	50g
Gluten-free starter	80g

Method: Day 1

Mix all three ingredients together in a bowl. Once combined, cover with cling film and leave at room temperature overnight.

Day 2 ingredients

Tepid water	350g
Your choice of flour and starch combination	400g
Fine sea salt	10g
Olive oil (for bowl)	50g

Method: Day 2

1. Combine the water and poolish and give a good stir, then add to the rest of the ingredients and combine.
2. Cover and leave at room temperature for four hours, until the dough has firmed up enough to enable you to pull it from the sides of the bowl, and drizzle the olive oil around the inside of the bowl.
3. Cover and leave in the fridge overnight.

Method: Day 3

1. The dough will have continued to prove during the night, and there should be good fermentation activity. Preheat the oven to 220°C/gas mark 7. Line a baking tray with baking parchment and slide the dough on to it – the olive oil should make this easier.

2. Pour the remainder of the olive oil on to the dough and gently make dimples in the dough with your fingers. Add the toppings of your choice – for example, a little flaked sea salt and rosemary – and put the tray into the oven, adding a spritz of water before closing the door. Bake for 25–30 minutes, remembering not to open the door.

3. Once the focaccia has been baked, add a good glug of olive oil and enjoy.

Sourdough pizza topped with vegetarian ingredients.

GLUTEN-FREE SOURDOUGH PIZZA

Makes two

Ingredients

Water	270g
Ground potato starch	5g
Teff flour	5g
Ground chia seed	1 tbsp
Salt	6g
Gluten-free starter	100g
Your choice of flour and starch combination	228g
Olive oil	1 tbsp

Method

1. Combine the first four ingredients in a medium bowl and whisk quickly until a thick gel forms.
2. Add salt and again mix until thoroughly combined.
3. Add starter and mix thoroughly.
4. Next, add the flour and stir until it is well incorporated, then add the oil, stirring until combined. Cover and leave to ferment for approximately four hours at room temperature.
5. After the fermentation, the dough will be slightly puffed up, but will not have increased as much as double in size. Preheat oven to as hot as it will go; use a pizza stone or an upside-down baking tray and get this nice and hot.
6. Take two pieces of parchment paper big enough for the pizzas and divide the dough in two. Put one piece of dough on each parchment paper and with wet hands shape the dough into the desired pizza shape, creating a ridge for a crust.
7. When the oven has preheated, carefully lift the parchment, with the crust on it, on to the pizza stone. Next, close the oven door most of the way and then carefully use a spray bottle to spray water on the side of the oven wall. Alternatively, pop three of four ice cubes in the bottom of the oven to produce a little steam. After doing this, quickly close the door the rest of the way.
8. Bake for about 5–7 minutes or until it has finished rising but is not completely browned. Take out of the oven and top as desired.
9. Put back in the oven to finish baking until the crust is golden and the cheese is bubbling.

I truly believe that the tastiest and healthiest gluten-free breads are made in the home. Many of the gluten-free products available from the supermarkets have a high level of sugar, as manufacturers try to add 'interest' to a bread that has had a reputation for a lack of flavour.

In my opinion, changing your bread into a sourdough will give you all the flavour you need. I gave a home-baked chia and linseed loaf to a friend without mentioning that it was gluten-free, and a few weeks later he asked for the recipe, as his family had really loved it. He was astonished to learn that it was gluten-free. Don't wait for the industry to catch up; become your own product developer!

CHAPTER 5

SOURDOUGH: A LIFESTYLE CHOICE

This chapter will explore in more detail the benefits of sourdough, and explain why it is not only a tastier, but also a healthier lifestyle choice.

Unquestionably, the taste of a sourdough is far superior to that of a supermarket bread. The wild yeast's perfect marriage with the lactobacillus allows the fermentation process to build complex flavours, at a slower rate. The time put into a sourdough builds these flavours gradually, to provide a bread that is quite capable of evoking passion in the person who gets to eat it. Because of the proving rate, time has been slowed down. This, combined with a higher hydration level, builds a denser, chewier and more open crumb; it is a slice with more substance than its mass-produced cousins.

Mass production of bread aims to speed up the process, with the aid of sugars and industrial provers, in order to maximize yield and profit. The sugars provide extra food for the baker's yeast to rapidly multiply, and the provers provide the perfect heat and humidity conditions to amplify productivity. This process allows the production of a low-cost bread that is frequently, within the industry, referred to as a 'sandwich carrier'; the terminology says it all!

SOURDOUGH FERMENTATION AND ITS BENEFITS

Sourdough fermentation is one of the oldest food biotechnologies. It has been studied and recently rediscovered for its effect on the sensory, structural, nutritional and shelf-life properties of leavened baked goods. Acidification, proteolysis and activation of a number of enzymes, as well as the synthesis of microbial metabolites, cause several changes during sourdough fermentation.

The current literature is particularly rich, with results showing how sourdough fermentation may affect the nutritional and functional features of leavened baked goods. In the form of pre-treating raw materials, fermentation through sourdough may stabilize or increase the functional value of bran fractions and wheatgerm. Sourdough fermentation may decrease the glycaemic response of baked goods, improve the properties and bioavailability of dietary fibre complex and phytochemicals, and may increase the uptake of minerals. Microbial metabolism during sourdough fermentation may also produce new nutritionally active compounds, such as peptides and amino acid derivatives (for example, amino butyric acid) with various functionalities, and potentially prebiotic exo-polysaccharides. The wheat flour digested via fungal proteases and selected sourdough lactobacilli has been demonstrated very likely to be safe for coeliac patients (according to Marco Gobbetti of the Department of Soil, Plant and Food Science, University of Bari, Italy).

OTHER FERMENTED FOODS

Fermentation is the bacterial (or yeast) conversion of sugar and starch to acids and other by-products, including ethanol. The acidity prevents the growth of food spoilage bacteria and fermentation has been used as a food preservation method for thousands of years. It also creates foods with a unique sour, tangy flavour.

Fermented products such as yogurt, beer and bread are increasingly popular, and more frequently available on supermarket shelves, alongside fermented foods traditionally consumed in other parts of the world for many centuries. These include sauerkraut ('sour cabbage') in Germany, kombucha in China, kimchi in Korea, and kefir in the Caucasian mountains. (It is worth noting that products that are subsequently processed by heat, baking or filtration (for example, pasteurized sauerkraut or sourdough) inactivate or remove the microbes in fermented foods, and so will not contain live cultures.)

Potential Benefits

The potential benefits of fermented foods have been widely heralded in the popular media. The main area of research with regards to their health benefits is in the probiotic content; probiotics are defined as live micro-organisms that can become established within the gut and confer a benefit to the host. Although there are currently no authorized European health claims for probiotics, there is a growing recognition of the importance of the gut microbiota, both for gut and non-gut health outcomes.

However, the beneficial effects of probiotics are strictly strain-specific and the strain composition and stability of the microbes in fermented foods are not well understood. Experts have concluded that fermented foods with unidentified microbial content cannot be considered probiotics. Furthermore, it is not always possible to distinguish clearly the potential contribution of the microbial content from that of the food matrix – in other words, the health benefit could be associated with other aspects of the food, rather than the microbes.

Scientific Evidence

A number of *in-vitro* and animal studies, using fermented foods such as sauerkraut and kombucha, report encouraging results. But more detailed reading indicates that researchers often use an extracted fraction of the fermented food or an isolated bacterial strain from them. Furthermore, there is only a limited evidence base for a relationship between fermented foods and health in humans. In cohort studies, yogurt and other fermented dairy foods have been associated with health benefits; however, no causal links can be drawn from this type of study. A very small number of controlled human trials using kimchi, kefir and other fermented dairy products have reported improvements in some health parameters.

Use of sourdough is increasingly interesting for the improvement of flavour, structure and stability in baked goods. Cereal fermentations also show significant potential in improving the nutritional quality and health effects of foods and ingredients. In addition to improving the sensory quality of wholegrain, fibre-rich or gluten-free products, sourdough can also actively retard starch digestibility leading to low glycaemic responses, modulate levels and bio-accessibility of bioactive compounds, and improve mineral bioavailability. Cereal fermentation may produce non-digestible polysaccharides or modify accessibility of the grain fibre complex to gut microbiota. It has also been suggested that degradation of gluten may render bread better suitable for coeliac persons, as previously stated.

The changes in the cereal matrix potentially leading to improved nutritional quality are numerous. Acid production, as well as possibly retarding starch digestibility, may also adjust pH to a range that favours the action of certain endogenous enzymes, thus changing the bioavailability pattern of minerals and phytochemicals. This is especially beneficial in products rich in bran, to deliver minerals and potentially protective compounds in the blood circulation. The action of enzymes during fermentation also causes hydrolysis and solubilization of grain macromolecules, such as proteins and cell wall polysaccharides. This changes the product texture, which may affect nutrient and non-nutrient absorption. New bioactive compounds, such as prebiotic oligosaccharides or other metabolites, may also be formed in cereal fermentations (according to the VTT Technical Research Centre of Finland).

FLOUR CHOICES

When it comes to discovering tastier and healthier options, the first thing to do is to experiment with flour combinations. With a range of fantastic-tasting flours now widely available, the choice has never been better for bakers. One way to explore the availability of various flours is to source a local mill and talk to the miller about flour and various flour combinations. Most millers will welcome visitors with open arms, and new mills are popping up everywhere with the resurgence in sourdough and artisan baking. One such mill is Wright's Flour in Ponders End, London, a family-run business that was started by George Reynolds Wright in 1867. It is run today by George's great-great-grandson David Wright. The mill has gone through many changes since it opened, but it maintains a strong sense of family and community. David's dedication to the

Wright's flour mill.

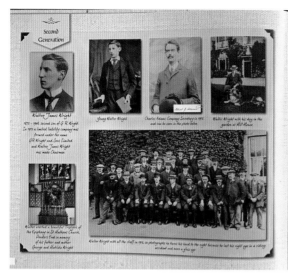

Building the gluten structure with low-protein flour.

Komo flour mill.

history of the mill and his passion for sourcing local grains are evident; he really values the relationship he has with all the farmers who supply him with grain:

> The relationship we have with our suppliers is paramount. It's not only about giving the farmer an honest price for their hard work, it's about helping each other through the hard times, such as a bad harvest. These are not just suppliers; these are our friends!

Small-scale grain producers are today growing a wider range of grain varieties. This new diversity, along with flour millers processing the grains using more traditional milling styles, has resulted in rich and flavourful flours that are shaking up the bread and baking business.

MILLING AT HOME

Sourcing your flour locally from a family-run business is a great option, but if you want complete control, why not become your own miller and mill your grains at home? This is a way of maintaining all the nutritional content in the bread, and is therefore a fantastic health choice. When grinding your own flour, the end result is a nutritious wholewheat product where nothing has been removed. It will contain more nutrients because it will retain the complete endosperm – the bran and germ will not have been sifted out, as they are in the production of white flour. For the gluten-intolerant, it will lessen the chance of cross-contamination.

There is a wide range of home milling machines available now, either hand-operated or electric. You could also contact the farmers directly and build a relationship; who knows better about grains than the people who grow them?

When the grains go into the hopper and come out again as powdery flour, you will know exactly what is being produced, because you will know what you have put in it. You can be confident that you are baking and feeding your family with nutritious flour with no fillers or additives. A wide variety of grains, beans, seeds and nuts can be ground into flour using your home grain mill. These include wheat, rye, corn, rice, barley, oats,

buckwheat, millet, kamut, quinoa, peas, mung beans, garbanzos and lentils.

Raw wheat berries are the hulled whole kernels of wheat. These can be used to make home-milled flours, or they can be cooked or left out to sprout (soak them in water and dry them off, then re-soak for around 24–48 hours). Grains can be white, russet, purple, or amber in colour. Spelt, kamut, emmer and einkorn are also available as whole grains. Even popcorn can be ground down to use in bread, providing a very interesting texture and flavour.

ADDITIONS TO AID DIGESTION

There is a full range of ancient grains to experiment with, along with an array of multi-seeds to include into sourdough bread. The increased presence of fibre will be massively helpful in aiding digestion in the gut, while the consumer's taste buds will appreciate the added benefit of flavour impact. Try researching and experimenting with different flours to personalize your sourdoughs; this will take some time, as most of the ancient grains are low in protein and the hydration levels of the dough will need to be adjusted. It will certainly help you evolve into a competent baker. The following are a few recipe examples to start the creative process.

• •

FARMHOUSE SEEDED SOURDOUGH

Day 1 ingredients	
Strong white flour	50g
Water (at hand warm temp., 32–37°C)	50g
Active wheat starter	100g
Sunflower seeds	35g
Pumpkin seeds	35g
Golden flax seeds	35g
Sesame seeds	15g
Olive oil	1 tbsp
Water (for seeds)	335g

Close-up of farmhouse seeded loaf.

Method: Day 1

1. Mix the flour and water by hand with the whole quantity of the starter, ensuring that both flour and starter are evenly distributed throughout the mix. Leave loosely covered at room temperature overnight.

2. Meanwhile, soak the seeds in the water and leave at room temperature overnight.

Day 2 ingredients

Starter from Day 1	100g
Water and seed mix from Day 1	
Strong white flour	335g
Wholemeal flour	75g
Rye flour	40g
Salt	8g
Extra seeds for topping	228g

Method: Day 2

1. In a large bowl combine the recipe starter with the water and seeds, and mix gently until it is even. In another bowl combine the three flours and the salt.

2. Add the flour mix (the dry ingredients) to the first bowl and mix using one hand until a dough mass is formed. (Keep the other hand clean for using utensils, and so on.) This will take only a couple of minutes. Use a plastic dough scraper around the bowl to make sure all the flour is mixed in. Cover the bowl with a shower cap or damp tea towel and leave it to rest at room temperature.

3. After 5–10 minutes, give the dough a fold in the bowl, using slightly wet hands to prevent it sticking. Pull a section of the dough out to the side and fold it into the middle of the ball. Repeat this going around the ball of dough until getting back to the starting point (four or five folds). Use the scraper to turn the dough upside down, cover the bowl and leave for another 5–10 minutes.

4. Repeat these steps three more times. After the final fold, cover the bowl once more and leave to rest for one hour at room temperature.

5. Turn the dough out of the bowl on to a lightly floured surface. Stretch out one side of the dough and fold it into the middle. Repeat this with each of the four 'sides' of the dough.

6. Put the dough back in the bowl upside down and leave to rest for another hour at room temperature.

7. To shape a round loaf, once the dough has rested, turn it out on to a lightly floured surface. Stretch one side of the dough out and fold it into the middle. Repeat this all around the outside of the dough until you get back to your starting point. Flip it so the seam side is facing down. Use your left hand to hold the dough in place and your right hand to rotate the dough, tucking it under and tightening it as you go around. (If you are left-handed, you might want to use your right hand to stabilize and your left hand to rotate.) The idea here is to increase the strength of the dough without tearing it. The final surface of the dough should feel taut to the touch.

8. Put the remaining seeds in a bowl. Brush the top of the dough with water and carefully, but confidently, dunk it in the seeds so that they are evenly distributed over the top.

9. Place the dough so that the seam is facing up and the seeds face down in a round proving basket. There is no need to flour the basket as the layer of seeds will prevent the dough from sticking. At this stage place the dough into the fridge for an overnight prove.

10. To test whether the dough has proved enough, press your finger about 2–3cm into it, then remove. If the dough pushes back out slowly, it is ready. If it springs back quickly, the dough is under-proved; if it does not spring back at all, it is over-proved. Re-shape it and leave out at room temperature until it is at optimum prove.

11. Preheat the oven to 250°C/fan 240°C/gas mark 10 or the highest temperature on your model. Place a roasting dish in the bottom of the oven to heat up, and a flat baking tray on one of the shelves. Fill a cup with water and place to one side ready to use.

12. When the oven is up to temperature, take the hot baking tray out and carefully place it on a heat-resistant surface. Lightly dust it with flour and then turn the dough from the proving basket out on to the tray, slowly and smoothly.

13. Slash the dough with a sharp knife, using one quick, smooth action, to give a nice clean line; do not 'saw' at it. In the bakery, we use a single diagonal slash down the loaf, but there are endless variations; this is an opportunity to be creative and come up with your own distinctive pattern.

14. Place the baking tray in the oven and pour the cup of water into the preheated roasting dish at the bottom. The moisture created will make the dough lighter, help to set the crust and give it a lovely sheen.

15. Turn the temperature down to 240°C/fan 220°C/gas mark 9 and bake for 30–35 minutes. To check whether the bread is baked through, tap the bottom – it should sound hollow.

16. Leave the bread to cool for at least an hour before eating.

Method: Day 1

1. Mix half the quantity of the flours and half the quantity of the water with the whole quantity of the starter, leaving out the salt. Work the mixture evenly together and leave loosely covered at room temperature overnight.

2. Soak the seeds in the water and leave at room temperature overnight.

Method: Day 2

1. In a large bowl add the remaining flours and salt, then add the Day 1 recipe to this with the remaining water, seeds and mix gently.

2. Using one hand, mix until a dough is formed – this will take only a couple of minutes. (Keep the other hand clean for using utensils, and so on.) Use a plastic dough scraper around the bowl to make

EIGHT-SEED SOURDOUGH

Ingredients

Strong white bread flour	670g
Semolina	150g
Stoneground whole wheat	60g
Water	580g
Sea salt	19g
Sourdough starter	260g
Golden flax seeds	25g
Toasted sesame seeds	25g
Fennel seeds	7g
Raw sunflower seeds	20g
Poppy seeds	10g
Red quinoa seeds	10g
Hemp seeds	10g
Teff seeds	10g

Make a separate seed combination of the eight seeds (5g each =40g for seed topping)

Seeded loaves going into the oven.

sure all the flour is mixed in. Cover the bowl with a shower cap or damp tea towel and leave the dough to rest at room temperature.

3. After 5–10 minutes, give the dough a fold in the bowl, using slightly wet hands to prevent it sticking. Pull a section of the dough out to the side and fold it into the middle of the ball. Repeat this going around the ball of dough until you get back to the beginning (four or five folds). Use the scraper to turn the dough upside down, cover the bowl and leave for another 5–10 minutes.

4. Repeat these steps three times. After the final fold, cover the bowl again and leave to rest for one hour at room temperature.

Close-up image of seed inclusions.

5. Turn the dough out of the bowl on to a lightly floured surface. Stretch out one side of the dough and fold it into the middle. Repeat this with each of the four 'sides' of the dough. Put the dough back in the bowl upside down and leave to rest for another hour at room temperature.

6. To shape a round loaf, once the dough has rested, turn it out on to a lightly floured surface. Stretch one side of the dough out and fold it into the middle. Repeat this all around the outside of the dough until you get back to your starting point. Flip it so the seam side is facing down. Use your left hand to hold the dough in place and use your right hand to rotate the dough, tucking it under and tightening it as you go around. (If you are left-handed, you might want to use your right hand to stabilize and your left hand to rotate.) The idea here is to increase the strength of the dough without tearing it. The final surface of the dough should feel taut to the touch.

7. Put the remaining seeds in a bowl. Brush the top of the dough with water and dunk it in the seeds so that they are evenly spread over the top. Place the dough in a round proving basket, with the seam facing up and the seeds down. There is no need to flour the basket, as the seeds will prevent the dough from sticking. Place it in the fridge for an overnight prove.

8. To test whether the dough has proved enough, press your finger about 2–3cm into it, then remove. If the dough pushes back out slowly, it is ready. If it springs back quickly, the dough is under-proved; if it does not spring back at all, it is over-proved. Re-shape it and leave out at room temperature until it is at optimum prove.

9. Preheat the oven to 250°C/fan 240°C/gas mark 10 or the highest temperature on your model. Place a roasting dish in the bottom of the oven to heat up, and a flat baking tray on one of the shelves. Fill a cup with water and place to one side ready to use.

10. When the oven is up to temperature, take the hot baking tray out, lightly dust it with flour and then turn the dough from the proving basket out on to the tray. Slash the dough with a sharp knife, using one quick, smooth action to give a clean line; do not 'saw' at the dough. In the bakery, we use a single diagonal slash down the loaf, but there are endless variations; this is an opportunity to be creative and come up with your own distinctive pattern.

11. Place the baking tray in the oven and pour the cup of water into the preheated roasting dish at the bottom. The moisture created will make the dough lighter, help to set the crust and give it a lovely sheen.

12. Turn the temperature down to 240°C/fan 220°C/gas mark 9 and bake for 30–35 minutes. To check if the bread is baked through, tap the bottom – it should sound hollow.

13. Leave the bread to cool for at least an hour before eating.

• •

ANCIENT GRAINS AND SEEDS SOURDOUGH

Day 1: Stiff starter ingredients

Sourdough starter	40g
Water	17g
Einkorn flour	40g

Method: Day 1

1. Add the starter to the water and break down into a milky consistency. Add this to the flour and combine the ingredients together to form a stiff ball.

Day 2 ingredients

Stiff starter from Day 1	95g
Water	800g
Amaranth seeds	30g
Chia seeds	30g
Einkorn flour	500g
Emmer flour	250g
Buckwheat flour	250g
Salt	22g

Ancient seed and grain additions.

2. Cover the bowl with cling film and leave overnight at room temperature.

Method: Day 2

1. In a large bowl combine the stiff starter with the water and seeds and mix gently. In another bowl combine flours and the salt.

2. Add the flour mix to the first bowl and mix using one hand until a dough is formed. (Keep the other hand clean for using utensils, and so on.) This will take only a couple of minutes. Use a plastic dough scraper around the bowl to make sure all the flour is mixed in. Cover the bowl with a shower cap or damp tea towel and leave it to rest at room temperature.

3. After 5–10 minutes, give the dough a fold in the bowl, using slightly wet hands to prevent it sticking. Pull a section of the dough out to

the side and fold it into the middle of the ball. Repeat this going around the ball of dough until you get back to the beginning (four or five folds). Use the scraper to turn the dough upside down, cover the bowl and leave for another 5–10 minutes.

4. Repeat these steps three times. After the final fold, cover the bowl again and leave to rest for one hour at room temperature.

5. Turn the dough out of the bowl on to a lightly floured surface. Stretch out one side of the dough and fold it into the middle. Repeat this with each of the four 'sides' of the dough.

6. Put the dough back in the bowl upside down and leave to rest for another hour at room temperature.

7. To shape a round loaf, once the dough has rested, turn it out on to a lightly floured surface. Stretch one side of the dough out and fold it into the middle. Repeat this all around the outside of the dough until you get back to your starting point. Flip it so the seam side is facing down. Use your left hand to hold the dough in place and use your right hand to rotate the dough, tucking it under and tightening it as you go around. (If you are left-handed, you might want to use your right hand to stabilize and your left hand to rotate.) The idea here is to increase the strength of the dough without tearing it. The final surface of the dough should feel taut to the touch.

8. Put the remaining seeds in a bowl. Brush the top of the dough with water and dunk it in the seeds so that they are evenly spread over the top. Place the dough in a round proving basket, with the seam facing up and the seeds facing down. There is no need to flour the basket as the layer of seeds will prevent the dough from sticking. Place it in the fridge for an overnight prove.

9. To test whether the dough has proved enough, press your finger about 2–3cm into it, then remove. If the dough pushes back out slowly, it is ready. If it springs back quickly, the dough is under-proved; if it does not spring back at all, it is over-proved. Re-shape it and leave out at room temperature until it is at optimum prove.

10. Preheat the oven to 250°C/fan 240°C/gas mark 10 or the highest temperature on your model. Place a roasting dish in the bottom of the oven to heat up, and a flat baking tray on one of the shelves. Fill a cup with water and place to one side ready to use.

11. When the oven is up to temperature, take the hot baking tray out, lightly dust it with flour and then turn the dough from the proving basket out on to the tray. Slash the dough with a sharp knife, using one quick, smooth action to give a clean line; do not 'saw' at the dough. In the bakery, we use a single diagonal slash down the loaf, but there are endless variations; this is an opportunity to be creative and come up with your own distinctive pattern.

12. Place the baking tray in the oven and pour the cup of water into the preheated roasting dish at the bottom. The moisture created will make the dough lighter, help to set the crust and give it a lovely sheen.

13. Turn the temperature down to 240°C/fan 220°C/gas mark 9 and bake for 30–35 minutes. To check if the bread is baked through, tap the bottom – it should sound hollow.

14. Leave the bread to cool for at least an hour before eating.

SOURDOUGH BAKING: NOT JUST ABOUT THE BREAD

Sourdough bread is a fantastic creation and will enhance many a meal, but it is also possible to bring that same sour tang and texture combinations to other baked goods. The classic crumpet, for example, is a product yearning for a sour enhancement – it already possesses a classic aerated sourdough structure. It is also possible to introduce a sour element to sweet products such as muffins, biscuits, crispbreads and so on.

CHEESY SOURDOUGH CRUMPETS

Ingredients

Ingredients	
Sourdough starter	270g
Grated cheese	50g
Salt	3g
Bicarbonate of soda	½ tsp

Method

1. Combine the sourdough starter, cheese and salt together in a bowl and leave to rest until it starts to bubble up.

2. Prepare the crumpet rings (six 9cm moulds) by oiling the sides, and heat up a griddle pan or heavy-bottomed frying pan with a little oil on it. Keep it to a medium to low heat so as not to burn the crumpets. Place the rings in the pan.

3. Stir the bicarbonate of soda in to the batter mix and wait for it to bubble up. Pour the mix into the rings; fill them about half way, leaving space for the crumpets to rise. Cook for about 4–5 minutes until the top looks like it has dried out. The top will still look anaemic but do not be tempted to flip them over. Toast the final product until it is golden brown and then add lashings of butter.

Sourdough crumpet mixture.

ABOVE: **Use moulds to get the perfect crumpet shape and to retain the thick, chewy structure.**

BOTTOM: **The crumpets will bubble much like pancakes. The bubbles are proof that the mixture has pockets of sour air.**

Complete the crumpets with your choice of topping; a salty butter will complement the sourness well.

BLUEBERRY, CHOCOLATE AND POPPY SEED MUFFINS

Ingredients

Plain flour	156g
Light brown sugar	110g
Granulated sugar	67g
Baking powder	10g
Bicarbonate of soda	5g
Salt	2g
Sourdough starter	275g
Vegetable oil	70g
Sour cream	120g
Beaten egg	50g
Vanilla extract	4g
Frozen blueberries	230g
Chocolate chips	150g
Poppy seeds	15g

Method

1. Preheat oven to 190°C/fan 170°C/gas mark 5. Line a 12-cup muffin pan with parchment or paper liners.
2. In a large bowl, stir together the flour, sugars, baking powder, baking soda and salt. In a medium bowl, stir together the sourdough starter and oil until well combined. In a small bowl, stir together sour cream, egg and vanilla.
3. Add the blueberries to the sourdough mixture, whisking until incorporated.
4. Add the combination to the flour mixture, and fold to combine. Stir in chocolate chips and poppy seeds.
5. Spoon the batter into the prepared muffin cups, to two-thirds to three-quarters full.
6. Bake until they are lightly browned and a wooden pick inserted in the centre comes out clean (20–25 minutes).
7. Allow the muffins to cool in the pan for 10 to 15 minutes, then remove them and leave to cool on a wire rack.

SOURDOUGH PANCAKES

Ingredients

Whole milk	237ml
Plain flour	155g
Sourdough starter	118g
Vegetable oil	1 tbsp
Large egg	1
Salt	3g
Sugar	2 tbsp
Bicarbonate of soda	1 tsp
Butter	60g
Chocolate chips (optional)	

Method

1. In a large bowl, combine the milk, flour and sourdough starter. Let it sit for 30 minutes.
2. Preheat a greased cast-iron pan over a medium heat.
3. Add the rest of the ingredients to the milk, flour and sourdough mixture, and ensure they are whisked together well until light and airy with bubbles. It is best used straight away as it contains baking soda, which will activate immediately.
4. When the pan is hot, pour the batter into it – at this point, add a sprinkling of chocolate chips, if required – and cook until the edges appear dry and bubbles appear on the surface (about 3–4 minutes). Flip and cook for an additional 1–2 minutes until golden brown.
5. These pancakes are fabulous eaten hot with maple syrup and a little cinnamon sprinkled on top, or with butter, blueberries, ice cream, cream, or crispy streaky bacon.

LEFTOVERS

Leftover or stale sourdough – should there ever be any – has an array of uses. Sourdough bread has a long shelf life, with the acidity levels helping to kill off any potential mould spores, but it does eventually get less pliable. At this stage, it is time to breathe new life into it.

The first and most obvious transformation for leftover sourdough is bruschetta: a light toasting, a handful of nice mixed ripe tomatoes, a small bunch of fresh basil, sea salt, freshly ground black pepper, olive oil and a good quality white wine or herb vinegar will provide a real feast for the taste buds. Stale sourdough bread is also ideal for tossing into a sizzling pan of garlic-infused butter to make flavoursome croutons.

Alternatively, turn the sourdough bread into a perfect partner for hummus and other dips by making crispbread.

Crispbreads go perfectly with a cheeseboard.

SOURDOUGH CRISPBREADS

Ingredients

Ingredients	
Olive oil	15g
Caraway seeds	5g
Harissa paste	1 tsp
Slices of stale sourdough bread	2

Method

1. Stir the oil, caraway seeds and harissa paste together in a dish until combined.
2. De-crust the bread, place the slices between two pieces of parchment paper and with a rolling pin roll out as thin as you can.
3. Place the rolled-out bread on to a lined baking tray and lightly brush over the slices with the olive oil combination. Leave to soak in.
4. Preheat the oven to 200°C/fan 180°C/gas mark 6 and bake the slices for 8 minutes until crisp.
5. Leave to cool down fully and dry out, allowing the moisture to evaporate; the crispbreads are delicious with hummus or an olive tapenade.

Another firm favourite is the sourdough bread and butter pudding, which gives all the moisture back to the bread and infuses it with all the classic tangy tastes. This one is a must!

SOURDOUGH BREAD AND BUTTER PUDDING

Ingredients

Ingredients	
Slices of stale sourdough bread	5
Raisins	20g
Cinnamon	4g
Whole nutmeg	1
Egg yolks	3
Vanilla pod, split	1
Milk	300ml
Soft butter	50g
Eggs	3
Sugar	50g
Cream	300ml

Method

1. Butter the bread on both sides. Scatter the raisins into a dish and place the slices on top.
2. Mix the remaining ingredients, except the nutmeg, in a bowl and pour over the bread. Dunk the bread slices a few times to fully soak and saturate them.
3. Let the pudding sit for 20 minutes before baking.
4. Just before baking, grate the nutmeg over the dish. Put into the oven at a low temperature (around 120°C/248°F/gas mark ½) for 30 minutes, or until the custard has set.
5. Serve whilst still warm.

SHARPHAM PARK

1kg e

SPELT
FLOUR
ORGANIC GRAIN

WHOLEMEAL

Buckwheat flo

A stoneground flour mil
from wholegrain buckw
which is grown store
processed adjacent to
other cereals. Tradi
for pancakes and

EXPERTISE

1892

linso
TRONG WHITE
BREAD
FLOUR

NG YOU A BETTER B

O EASY BREAD
DEAL FOR
ite bloomer loaves
king & bread makers

DOVES FARM
EST. 1978

ORGANIC
Stoneground from wheat grain
widely used in prehistory,
this flour will give taste and
character to your baking.

ENGLISH WHOLEMEAL

Einkorn flour

GB · ORG · 05
EU Agriculture

DOVES FARM
EST. 1978

DOVES FARM
EST. 1978

WHOLEMEAL

Rye flour

ORGANIC
Stoneground from whole grain
this 100% rye flour is naturally
low in gluten, producing close
textured bread and cakes with a
pleasing continental flavour.

Rye grain has been
many years and
downlands. Tra
not suitabl
whea
woul
co
ch

GB · ORG · 03
EU Agriculture

CHAPTER 6

MODIFICATIONS

Most people's first steps into baking come by way of an innate human desire to make bread. This is usually followed by a recipe being passed down the family, or an idea in a baking book or on television catching the eye. Sure, the early days of the baking journey can be a little tricky – the desire to add a little more flour is very strong in the beginning, and it takes a little time and practice to master the mystical art of knowing when the dough is fully proved. Once gluten structure and optimum prove are properly understood, the baker is in a position to build and develop new recipes. The perfect loaf for each individual may not exist, so a knowledge of the 'baker's percentage' is a must at this stage.

THE 'BAKER'S PERCENTAGE'

In a recipe based on the 'baker's percentage', all the ingredients are calculated in relation to the total amount of flour within the recipe. To start with, the total amount of flour is denoted as 100%. This amount must account for all the flour used in a recipe – including all the different types, as well as the flour in any pre-ferment. The baker's percentage is then the amount of the ingredients in proportion to the amount of flour.

Examples

This example will enable you to perform a lot of helpful calculations, quickly determining the right amounts for all ingredients. A typical straightforward recipe may look like the following:

Ingredient	Percentage
Flour	100%
Water	63%
Salt	1.8%
Dry yeast	1.4%
Butter	4%
Total dough	**170.2%**

As it is not possible to weigh to decimal places on conventional digital weighing scales, it may be necessary to round up or down, and the end result may add up to slightly below or above the desired weight. This is fine within +/- 2g.

Example one: Making six loaves of 750g each
To make six loaves of bread weighing 750g each, the ingredients are calculated as follows: 6 x 750 = 4500g of dough.

The first step is to calculate the amount that represents 1%. For this example recipe, the total ingredient weights must add up to 4500g, equal to 170.2% of the initial flour weight (*see* table above: all the percentages of all ingredients added up).

To get to 1%, you need to divide 4500 by 170.2 = 26.44g.

So, each 1% represents **26.44g**. Therefore, by multiplying all percentages in the above table by 26.44g (1% of the desired weight), you get the following recipe, rounded to the nearest whole-numbered weight on a conventional digital weighing scale:

Ingredient	Calculation	Total
Flour (100%)	100 x 26.44g	2644g
Water (63%)	63 x 26.44g	1666g
Salt (1.8%)	1.8 x 26.44g	48g
Dry yeast (1.4%)	1.4 x 26.44g	37g
Butter (4%)	4 x 26.44g	106g
Total dough (170.2%)	**170.2 x 26.44g**	**4500g**

Example two: Making 12 loaves of 250g each
As with the first example, it is necessary to calculate the weight of the total dough, as follows: 12 x 250g = 3000g.

Again, this total weight is equal to 170.2% of the original flour weight. Therefore, the calculation is as follows: 1% = 3000/170.2% = 17.63g.

This gives the following recipe:

Ingredient	Calculation	Total
Flour (100%)	100 x 17.63g	1763g
Water (63%)	63 x 17.63g	1111g
Salt (1.8%)	1.8 x 17.63g	32g
Dry yeast (1.4%)	1.4 x 17.63g	25g
Butter (4%)	4 x 17.63g	71g
Total dough (170.2%)	**170.2 x 17.63g**	**3001g**

Example three: Making four loaves of 500g each
This example assumes you have found a nice recipe in a bread book, but, instead of using the amounts given in the recipe, you want to make four loaves of 500g each.

The recipe from the book is as follows:

Bread ingredients	
Wholewheat flour	50g
Flour	400g
Water	298g
Salt	8g
Dry yeast	6g

First of all, you need to calculate the total amount of flour in the original recipe (50g wholewheat + 400g white = 450g). With this number, you can now calculate all the baker's percentages of the recipe.

First, take 1% of the total amount of flour, which is 450 divided by 100 = 4.5g.

Now, divide all the weights of the initial recipe by 4.5, to calculate the baker's percentages.

Ingredient		Baker's percentage
Wholewheat flour	50g	50 ÷ 4.5 = 11%
Flour	400g	400 ÷ 4.5 = 89%
Water	298g	298 ÷ 4.5 = 66%
Salt	8g	8 ÷ 4.5 = 1.78%
Dry yeast	6g	6 ÷ 4.5 = 1.33%
Total dough	**762g**	**762 ÷ 4.5 = 169.1%**

Using this table, it is possible to scale the recipe to bake four loaves, as in Examples one and two. The total amount of dough needed is 4 x 500g = 2000g.

The total percentage of this recipe is 169.1%, so take 1% as 2000/169.1 = 11.83g.

Ingredient	Calculation	Total
Wholewheat flour (11%)	11 x 11.83g	130g
Flour (89%)	89 x 11.83g	1053g
Water (66%)	66 x 11.83g	781g
Salt (1.78%)	1.78 x 11.83g	21g
Dry yeast (1.33%)	1.33 x 11.83g	16g
Total dough (169.1%)	**169.1 x 11.83**	**2001g**

ADDING INCLUSIONS

When adding inclusions such as nuts, seeds, fruits and cheeses into the equation, a good rule of thumb is 10–15%. They should be incorporated after the dough has developed its gluten structure. This process is not to be confused with kneading; it is just a gentle folding, making sure the inclusions are evenly distributed. This gentle approach is particularly important when adding cheeses; if the dough is worked too hard, this will release the fat content of the cheese into the structure of the dough, resulting in a homogenized cheese flavour. Although this may not sound too bad, it is much better to come across a nice lump of stilton suspended in the crumb, as opposed to an overriding cheesy tinge.

Adding seed inclusions is pretty simple, unless you decide to soak them overnight. If the seeds or fruits are being soaked for the bread, use a percentage of the water from the dough recipe the day before, to keep the integrity of the recipe's proportions intact.

CONVERTING A YEASTED BREAD INTO A SOURDOUGH

By now sourdough is firmly on the radar and the desire to change all great recipes into a sourdough will be burning. The next section will provide the tools to convert a commercial yeasted product into a sourdough variant. With the understanding of the differing techniques that come with building a sourdough opposed to the yeasted method, that is bulk ferment and the folds to build a good strong structure, this will be easier than you think.

When looking at a yeasted recipe ripe for converting, concentrate on the flour weight and work out what 30% of that flour weight is. This will give you the amount in grams of the sourdough starter needed for conversion. Using the 30% as a bench mark for all recipe conversions will change a baker into a recipe developer, rather than a recipe follower.

• •

CONVERSION: CLASSIC ENGLISH LOAF INTO SOURDOUGH

This very simple classic may be deconstructed as follows (the method may be used as a template for converting any recipe):

Classic English loaf ingredients	Converted into sourdough
500g strong white bread flour	30% = 150g starter; use 250g for pre-ferment (50%)
40g soft butter	
12g fast-action dried yeast	Discard from the recipe
Salt	10g
300g water	Use 150g for pre-ferment (50%)

First, work out what 30% of the flour weight is (150g). This gives the amount of the starter needed to generate the carbon dioxide and the acidity levels for the conversion. Now it is time to start thinking like an artisan baker in terms of a pre-ferment.

Method: Day 1, the pre-ferment

1. Use 250g (50%) of the flour and 150g (50%) of the water from the recipe, and add a 150g sourdough starter to this mixture: this is now a pre-ferment. Combine it, then cover it and leave it at room temperature overnight.

2. The addition of 150g of starter will potentially cause a problem, as it will throw out the yield and hydration levels. However, it is easily remedied because the quantities of the white flour and water used in the pre-ferment are 50% of the original. This still means that a reduction is needed from the remaining recipe, to be added to the pre-ferment on Day 2.

3. As there is 150g extra, this must be divided by two and that weight must be removed from both the flour and the water additions. 150g/2 = 75g, so 75g of water and flour must be removed from the remaining weights:
The original flour weight = 500g – 50% (250g for the pre-ferment) = 250g – extra 75g = 175g flour to continue.
The original water weight = 300g – 50% (150g for the pre-ferment) = 150g – extra 75g = 75g water.

Method: Day 2, the final recipe (after deductions)

Ingredients	
Strong white bread flour	175g
Soft butter	40g
Salt	10g
Water	75g
Pre-ferment:	
Starter	150g
Flour	250g
Water	150g

1. Add all the ingredients to the first bowl of the pre-ferment and mix using one hand until a dough forms. (Keep the other hand clean for using utensils, and so on.) This will take only a couple of minutes. Use a plastic dough scraper around the bowl to make sure all the flour is mixed in. Cover the bowl with a shower cap or damp tea towel and leave it to rest at room temperature.

2. After 5–10 minutes, give the dough a fold in the bowl, using slightly wet hands to prevent it sticking. Pull a section of the dough out to the side and fold it into the middle of the ball. Repeat this going around the ball of dough until you get back to the beginning (four or five folds). Use the scraper to turn the dough upside down, cover the bowl and leave for another 5–10 minutes.

3. Repeat this folding step three times. After the final fold, cover the bowl again and leave to rest for one hour at room temperature.

4. Turn the dough out of the bowl on to a lightly floured surface. Stretch out one side of the dough and fold it into the middle. Repeat this with each of the four 'sides' of the dough. Put the dough back in the bowl upside down and leave to rest for another hour at room temperature.

5. After an hour, remove the dough from the bowl and stretch one side of the dough out and fold it into the middle. Repeat this all around the outside of the dough until you get back to your starting point. Flip it so the seam side is facing down. Use your left hand to hold the dough in place and your

right hand to rotate the dough, tucking it under and tightening it as you go around. (If you are left-handed, you might want to use your right hand to stabilize and your left hand to rotate.) The idea here is to increase the strength of the dough without tearing it. The final surface of the dough should feel taut to the touch.

6. Oil a 1lb loaf tin and turn out the dough on to a lightly floured work surface.

7. Fold the top of the dough into the centre and tuck the sides into the centre. Now fold the bottom of the dough into the centre leaving a seam. Place the dough into the loaf tin seam side down, and place into the fridge for an overnight prove.

8. To test whether the dough has proved enough, press your finger about 2–3cm into it, then remove. If the dough pushes back out slowly, it is ready. If it springs back quickly, the dough is under-proved; if it does not spring back at all, it is over-proved. Re-shape it and leave out at room temperature until it is at optimum prove.

9. Preheat the oven to 240°C/fan 230°C/gas mark 9. Place a roasting dish in the bottom of the oven to heat up, and a flat baking tray on one of the shelves. Fill a cup with water and place to one side ready to use.

10. When the oven is up to temperature, transfer the loaf tin on to the baking tray. Place the tray in the oven and pour the cup of water into the preheated roasting dish at the bottom. The moisture created will make the dough lighter, help to set the crust and give it a lovely sheen.

11. Turn the temperature down to 220°C/fan 210°C/gas mark 9 and bake for 30–35 minutes. To check if the bread is baked through, tap the bottom – it should sound hollow.

12. Allow to cool at room temperature for one hour.

• •

HYDRATION LEVELS

With more experience and confidence, a baker can start to revisit hydration levels in recipes, taking the classic English loaf as a starting point, for example. The English loaf is developed to deliver a tight, soft crumb structure perfect for sandwich making. Respecting the hydration levels in the English loaf will result in a similar crumb structure. It will have some of the characteristics of a sourdough – sour taste profile, chewy crumb and added shelf life – but it will not deliver the classic sourdough aerated appearance.

The English loaf has a hydration level of 60% of the flour weight. The added fat content in the butter gives a little more hydration, but not close to what is needed to convert this recipe into a true sourdough. A baker developing a sourdough recipe needs to be looking at hydration levels of at least 75%. This is why the bulk fermentation process is so vital for strengthening the structure of a sourdough. As an example, ciabatta has a minimum hydration level of 85%; indeed, it can actually take more water than flour, up to 120% hydration. A high level of hydration, combined with bulk fermentation, results in an open crumb structure, and in ciabatta it is particularly dramatic, open and chewy.

CONVERTING A CROISSANT

It is also possible to make a poolish from an original yeasted product, for example, the classic croissant recipe, and adapt it into a sourdough product.

• •

CONVERSION: YEASTED CROISSANT INTO SOURDOUGH

Croissant ingredients	
Full fat milk	140g
Strong white bread flour	500g
Salt	12g
Caster sugar	55g
Dry yeast	15g
Unsalted butter	40g
Unsalted butter (for laminating)	250g
Water	140g

Triangles of croissant dough ready for rolling.

Buttery croissant layers.

First, make a poolish using ingredients from the original recipe.

Day 1: Poolish ingredients

Strong white bread flour	150g from original recipe
Water	65g from original recipe
Sourdough starter	150g (30% of original flour weight)

Method: Day 1, the poolish

Combine the ingredients together, cover and leave at room temperature overnight.

For the finished conversion recipe, subtract the weights used for the poolish, and 50% of the extra starter weight from the water and the flour; this will leave you with 0g of water to add at this point.

Day 2: Remaining ingredients

Poolish starter	
Full fat milk	140g
Strong white bread flour	275g
Salt	12g
Unsalted butter	40g
Unsalted butter (for laminating)	250g
Medium eggs	2

Method: Day 2, converted sourdough croissant

1. Warm the milk a little and add to the poolish. Add the rest of the ingredients, apart from the 250g quantity of butter, to the poolish mixture and bring together into a shaggy mass, trying not to work the gluten too much. Leave the dough covered at room temperature for two hours until there is a noticeable change in volume.

2. Roll the butter into a nice flat square. The easiest way to do this is to place it between two pieces of baking paper and pound it gently with a rolling pin until it is about ¼ inch thick, and 25cm x 25cm. Place it back in the fridge.

3. Take the dough and place it on to a floured work surface. Roll it out to form a square around 25cm, then roll out the top, bottom and each side a little extra – this will provide the flaps to enclose the butter. Leave a raised square platform of dough in the centre, manipulate the butter into the shape of the raised platform, brush any excess flour from the dough and place the butter on to the platform. Pull the top flap of the dough over the butter, making sure the flap provides full 100% coverage, then do the same with the bottom flap and with the side flaps, ensuring they meet in the middle.

4. Gently depress the dough with the rolling pin to help distribute the butter evenly, then roll it out up and down until it is 65cm long. Brush away any excess flour and fold the top half of the

dough into the centre; repeat with the bottom half. This whole procedure is one fold.

5. Wrap the dough in baking paper and place in the fridge for one hour.

6. Take the dough out of the fridge and turn out on to a floured work surface. Now imagine the dough represents the binding of a book and an open double page. Place the binding of the book on the left-hand side, gently depress it with the rolling pin and roll it out, following the same procedure as for the first fold. Again, return it to the fridge.

7. Repeat this process two more times, so that the dough has received four folds. This is the lamination process that will give the croissants the characteristic cross-sections of spirals.

8. To construct the croissants, take the dough out of the fridge and place on to a lightly floured surface. With the seam running side to side, roll the dough out so it is a generous half rolling pin long. Turn the dough so the seam is running top to bottom and roll it out until it is 50cm long and 25cm wide. It should be a bit less than ¼ inch thick.

9. Turn the dough so that you have a short wide rectangle in front of you. Then, with a sharp knife, cut it into 12 equal triangles. The base of each triangle should be roughly 4 fingers wide. Cut a small slit about ¼ inch long at the base of each triangle.

10. Gently stretch your triangle out, then roll up your croissant, making sure the tail is on the bottom of the rolled-up croissant. Place on to a tray lined with baking paper, ensuring they are evenly spaced out.

11. Whisk up the egg and spray or brush over each croissant.

12. Leave your croissants to rise in a warmish place (ideally at about 24°C) for roughly two hours. In this time, they should double in size and you will be able to see the layers you have so lovingly created. When they are ready to bake, they should also have a nice wobble to them. If they are not ready after two hours give them a bit longer – it will be worth the wait!

13. Preheat the oven to 210°C/fan 190°C/gas mark 7. Place the tray in the oven and lightly spritz the oven chamber with a water spray.
14. Bake for 12–15 minutes until they are a nice golden colour and slightly crispy on the outside.

• •

COMMERCIAL ENHANCERS

Making a sourdough is a natural approach to bread-making. However, it is widely understood that companies involved in the mass production of breads have a few tricks up their sleeve to ensure the consistency and shelf life of every loaf. It is good to be aware of some of the ingredients that are used in commercial breads.

Fat

Hard fats improve loaf volume and crumb softness and help the bread to last longer. Hydrogenated fats have commonly been used, although large bakeries are phasing them out. One option is to replace them with fractionated fats, which do not contain or produce the trans fats that have been associated with heart disease.

Flour Treatment Agent

L-ascorbic acid (E300) can be added to flour by the miller, or incorporated at the baking stage. It acts as an oxidant, helping to retain gas in the dough, which makes the loaf rise more and gives a false impression of value. It is not permitted in wholemeal flour but is permitted in wholemeal bread.

Bleach

Chlorine dioxide gas is used by millers to make white flour whiter. It has some 'improving' effect on the flour – bleaches have been used as a substitute for the natural ageing of flour.

Reducing Agent

Used as L-cysteine hydrochloride (E920), cysteine is a naturally occurring amino acid used in baking to create stretchier doughs, especially for burger buns and French sticks. It may be derived from animal hair and feathers.

Soya Flour

Widely used in bread 'improvers', soya flour has a bleaching effect on flour, and assists the machinability of dough and the volume and softness of bread, enabling more water to be added to the dough.

Emulsifiers

Widely used in bread improvers to control the size of gas bubbles, emulsifiers enable the dough to hold more gas and therefore grow bigger and make the crumb softer. Emulsifiers also reduce the rate at which the bread goes stale.

Preservatives

Calcium propionate is widely used in the mass production of bread, as is vinegar (acetic acid). Preservatives are necessary only for prolonged shelf life – home freezing is a chemical-free alternative.

NATURAL IMPROVERS

Baking with sourdough often results in a loaf or rolls that miss the mark on reproducible quality – they may be lacking in volume or the structure may be uneven – but every one can be passed off as 'artisan'! However, if you are seeking to improve on the consistency of your bakes, and guarantee a better success rate, you will need to consider adding improvers. Of course, a sourdough baker would not dream of adding anything from the commercial baker's list of improvers to aid consistency, but fortunately there are a number of natural options.

Apple Cider

Apple cider seems to be high on the radar with the health-conscious as an aid to weight loss. In bread-making, it lowers the pH of the dough, aiding with volume. It can be added at a level up to 1.25% of the amount of flour, but beyond that it will have an impact in terms of the taste of the finished bread. Acid also has a strengthening effect on the dough.

Diastatic Malt

Diastatic malt powder helps to promote a strong rise, great texture, and lovely brown crust. It is especially useful when flour does not have barley malt added, which is the case with most wholewheat flours and many organic flours. Active enzymes in diastatic malt help yeast grow fully and efficiently throughout the fermentation period, yielding a good, strong rise, and great oven spring.

Potato Starch

Potato starch can be included either in the form of mashed potato or the water left over from boiling potatoes. This can result in a softer crumb and a great oven spring, creating an exceptional volume in the bread. However, it may be necessary to make adjustments to the hydration levels of the basic recipe when using potato starch.

Old Dough

During a bake, sometimes there may be a little dough left over that will not fit into the plans. Old dough can provide a great improver for the next bake. If it is to be used within a couple of days, the spare dough can be kept in the fridge; otherwise, it can go into a Ziplock bag and into the freezer. Artisan bakeries will purposely develop a mix of dough and leave it in the chiller to use in future bakes.

The old dough will act as a taste improver, with all those flavours that have been gained during the fermentation process. It will also help with creating good volume in breads.

ADJUSTING SOURNESS

Increasing Sourness

There are two main acids produced in a sourdough culture – lactic acid and acetic acid – which give a sourdough its distinctive tang. Giving acetic acid-producing organisms optimal conditions in which to thrive and multiply will produce a tangier finished product. The first option is to maintain the starter at a lower hydration level, using a higher ratio of flour to water. Acetic acid is produced more readily in a drier environment, while lactic acid-producing organisms seem to thrive in a wet environment.

Other tactics to increase the tanginess include the following:

- Keeping the hooch (*see* page 29). Some bakers recommend throwing the hooch away, but keeping it will ensure a tangier flavour.
- Manipulating prove times can lead to a greater sour hit.
- Find a cooler spot for rising the dough, as this will help to slow down fermentation, allowing the flavours to build more.
- Punch back the dough at least once, if not twice, before the final shaping of the loaf.
- Perform the final prove for at least four hours, or overnight in the refrigerator.

Reducing Sourness

The tang of the final product can be reduced by feeding the starter more often. The temperature of the culturing area and the strength of the starter will influence how often it will need feeding – this can be anything from every eight hours to every 24 hours. Increasing the frequency of the feedings should create a milder taste, as it will minimize the alcohol content and reduce the overall acidity of the sourdough. Less acidity means less tang.

The sour taste can also be reduced by using more starter in the dough. A larger percentage of sourdough starter in the dough allows it to rise in a cooler location, and to have a shorter rising time. Both conditions help to restrict the sourness in sourdough by lowering the level of acetic acid.

Some bakers like to add a small amount of baking soda to neutralize some of the acidity, which will also give the dough a little extra volume.

CHAPTER 7

WORLDWIDE SOURDOUGHS

Globally, sourdough is a huge success story. From its ancient roots, by way of the horrors of modern technology and mass production, which almost led to its demise, it has enjoyed something of a renaissance in recent years.

Britain played a major role in the story of bread, with the development of the Chorleywood Process in the early 1960s, which used additives to create a soft, springy bread with a longer shelf life. In America, the equivalent was the national disgrace that was 'Wonder Bread'. Even France, with its impressive history of baking, did not get away scot-free in the mid-1970s!

America eventually redeemed itself by starting the Artisan Movement in California. The information age brought a better understanding of bread development and best practices. This, combined with a growth in the awareness of health and wellbeing, was a catalyst to bring back the old ways of baking. Inevitably, this included the sourdough process, which is simply a healthier and more naturalistic approach to baking.

Each country has its own unique sourdoughs. The variations come from the wheats and grasses available in each particular location, and the diversity can introduce the palate to some wonderful flavour combinations.

GERMAN BREADS

Germany must be the main contender in terms of sticking to their roots. In Germany, many areas are not conducive to wheat production, so grains such as rye and spelt tend to be more prevalent. German bakers were producing nutritious wholegrain bread long before the organic health food movement.

Brötchen (Bread Rolls)

This is a standard white bread roll. It is not known as Brötchen everywhere in Germany; some regions have their own word, including Semmeln, Wecken, Schrippen or Rundstück (literally the 'round piece'). There are also different variations of Brötchen with sesame, poppy or pumpkin seeds sold as wholegrain rolls.

Milchbrötchen (Milk Roll)

A variation of the roll made from fluffy white dough prepared with milk, often with raisins or chocolate chips added, making it a favourite for little Germans at the breakfast table.

Hörnchen

Another breakfast staple (especially on Sundays), Hörnchen or 'little horns' are the German version of croissants, albeit with more butter. Coming in a similar half-moon shape, Hörnchen are delicious with jam or even chocolate spread.

Vollkornbrot (Wholegrain Bread)

Most loaves on the shelves of German bakeries are of the dark brown and healthy variety, and wholegrain bread accounts for many of these. It is commonly eaten with cheese or cold meats in the evening, and it is actually protected by a law, which makes it mandatory for Vollkornbrot to have a wholegrain flour content of at least 90%.

Pumpernickel

One of the country's most famous breads, Pumpernickel is a rich dark bread made with 100% rye, originating in the northern areas of Germany. It is baked over a long period of time at low temperatures, and often served in hors d'oeuvres with cucumbers or fish. It is so popular that most supermarkets across Germany sell Pumpernickel in small, pre-sliced batches.

Roggenbrot (Rye Bread)

This covers literally any rye bread other than Pumpernickel. It varies a lot in density and colour, depending on regional recipes and preferences.

Katenbrot

This is another dark brown and coarsely textured wholegrain variety. Katenbrot means 'barn bread', and, like Vollkornbrot, is a staple on German dinner tables. It is best enjoyed with cheese and cold cuts.

Sonnenblumenbrot (Sunflower Seed Bread)

As the name suggests, this bread is sprinkled with a generous dose of sunflower seeds and tastes slightly sweet, making it a good healthy breakfast option. Try it with cream cheese and fruit jam – delicious!

Dreikornbrot/Fünfkornbrot (Three-/Five-Grain Bread)

These variations of wholegrain bread must be among the healthiest bread options in Germany. Made with variations of wheat, rye, barley, oats and maize, they can be eaten for breakfast, lunch and dinner, and are especially delicious served with soup.

Brezel (Pretzel)

This hearty speciality, sometimes sprinkled with salt, originates in the southern parts of Germany, where it is known as Brez'n.

● ●

BRÖTCHEN (BREAD ROLLS)

Poolish ingredients	
Strong white flour	200g
Water	75g
Sourdough starter	150g

Method: Day 1, the poolish

Place all the ingredients into a bowl, stir until fully incorporated, then cover with cling film and leave at room temperature overnight.

Brötchen ingredients	
Flour	225g
Water	150g
Sugar	1 tsp
Salt	5g
Semolina	50g
Poolish starter	

Method: Day 2

1. Add the poolish mixture to the recipe ingredients and work together with your hands until the dough is well combined. Bring the dough together into a ball.

2. Knead the dough on a clean work surface for 6–8 minutes, or until it is elastic and smooth.

3. After 5–10 minutes, give the dough a fold in the bowl, using slightly wet hands to prevent it sticking. Pull a section of the dough out to the side and fold it into the middle of the ball. Repeat this going around the ball of dough until you get back to the beginning (four or five folds). Use the scraper to turn the dough upside down, cover the bowl and leave for another 5–10 minutes.

4. Repeat this step three times. After the final fold, cover the bowl again and leave to rest for one hour at room temperature.

5. Turn the dough out of the bowl on to a lightly floured surface. Stretch out one side of the dough and fold it into the middle. Repeat this with each of the four 'sides' of the dough. Put the dough back in the bowl upside down and leave to rest for another hour at room temperature.

6. Stretch one side of the dough out and fold it into the middle. Repeat this all around the outside of the dough until you get back to your starting point. Flip it so the seam side is facing down. Use your left hand to hold the dough in place and your right hand to rotate the dough, tucking it under and tightening it as you go around. (If you

are left-handed, you might want to use your right hand to stabilize and your left hand to rotate.) The idea here is to increase the strength of the dough without tearing it. The final surface of the dough should feel taut to the touch.

7. Separate the mixture into eight parts and roll each into a ball. Flatten each one slightly with the palm of your hand and transfer the rolls on to a baking tray lined with a tea towel and dusted with semolina. Leave in the fridge overnight.

8. To test whether the dough has proved enough, press your finger about 2–3cm into it, then remove. If the dough pushes back out slowly, it is ready. If it springs back quickly, the dough is under-proved; if it does not spring back at all, it is over-proved.

9. Meanwhile, preheat the oven to 220°C/fan 210°C/gas mark 7. Place a roasting dish in the bottom of the oven to heat up. Fill a cup with water and place to one side ready to use.

10. Place the baking tray in the oven and pour the cup of water into the preheated roasting dish. The moisture created will make the dough lighter, help to set the crust and give it a lovely sheen.

11. When the rolls have expanded, dust them with semolina and transfer them to the oven. Bake for 12–15 minutes, or until golden brown and cooked through.

12. To serve, separate the rolls and serve warm with butter.

• •

ROGGENBROT

Pre-ferment ingredients

Rye flour	300g
Water	250g
Sourdough starter	190g

Method: Day 1, pre-ferment

Mix the flour, water and sourdough starter together and combine, then cover with cling film and leave overnight at room temperature.

Roggenbrot ingredients

Bread flour	245g
Water	105g
Salt	12g
Diastatic malt powder	7g
Barley malt syrup (or light molasses)	10g
Pre-ferment	
Semolina	50g

Method: Day 2

1. Add the pre-ferment to the recipe ingredients and combine.

2. The dough will be firm but sticky, so wet your hands to keep it from sticking too badly. Turn the dough on to a clean board and knead for 6-8 minutes for full gluten structure. Form into a ball, place in a bowl and cover with a damp cloth for 30 minutes at room temperature. You may see some rise.

3. Divide the dough into two parts and shape into boules.

4. Dust the prover baskets with semolina and place the dough into the baskets seam side up. Put the baskets into the fridge overnight.

5. To test whether the dough has proved enough, press your finger about 2–3cm into it, then remove. If the dough pushes back out slowly, it is ready. If it springs back quickly, the dough is under-proved; if it does not spring back at all, it is over-proved. Re-shape it and leave out at room temperature until it is at optimum prove.

6. Preheat the oven to 240°C/fan 230°C/gas mark 9. Place a roasting dish in the bottom of the oven to heat up, and a flat baking tray on one of the shelves. Fill a cup with water and place to one side ready to use.

7. When the oven is up to temperature, transfer the boules on to the baking tray and place the tray in the oven. Pour the cup of water into the preheated roasting dish at the bottom. The moisture created will make the dough lighter, help to set the crust and give it a lovely sheen.

8. Turn the temperature down to 220°C/fan 210°C/gas mark 9 and bake for 30–35 minutes. To check if the bread is baked through, tap the bottom – it should sound hollow.

9. Allow to cool at room temperature for one hour.

· ·

FRENCH BREADS

Bread is not just a food to the French; it represents so much more. No other country has had such a passionate love affair with it, combined with such levels of respect. Bread is ingrained in the fabric of the nation. The availability of bread has been guaranteed by law in the French capital since the chaotic days of the French Revolution, when bread shortages led to desperate measures among the Parisian poor – in October 1798 baker Denis François was lynched by an angry mob for not opening his shop. When Queen Marie Antoinette was told of the shortages, she is alleged to have angered the mob even more by declaring with some disdain that they should 'eat brioche', a more expensive bread enriched with butter and eggs.

Following the bloody overthrow of the French monarchy, the Constituent Assembly passed a military law allowing the authorities to commandeer bakeries and keep the masses in bread. The law was updated as recently as the 1950s, and now regulates bakers' summer holidays, thus avoiding a potentially dangerous shortage of the vital foodstuff. A French person's right to a fresh baguette is sacrosanct.

The baking techniques developed by the French have been copied by every artisan baker around the globe, for one good reason: because they are the best!

Pain de Campagne ('Country Bread')
This is typically a large round loaf ('miche').

Fougasse
A type of bread typically associated with Provence but found (with variations) in other regions. Some versions

Traditional French baguette.

are sculpted or slashed into a pattern resembling an ear of wheat.

Baguette

The classic French baguette (the name means 'stick') is made from a basic dough that must contain no more than four ingredients: flour, water, salt and yeast. Although the dough recipe is defined by French law, the shape is not. It is distinguishable by its length and its crisp crust. A baguette has a diameter of about 5 or 6cm and usually a length of about 65cm, although a baguette can be up to 1m long.

Sour air bubbles inside a baguette.

Close-up of sliced traditional baguette with sourdough structure inside.

Brioche

The brioche is more of a 'viennoiserie', in that it is made in the same basic way as bread, but has a richer taste and texture because of the addition of eggs, butter and liquid.

Pain au Levain

The French term for naturally leavened bread is generally considered to be the gold standard for wild yeast breads.

. . . .

PAIN DE CAMPAGNE

Stiff starter ingredients	
Sourdough starter	100g
Rye flour	40g
Water	60g

Method: Day 1, stiff starter

In a small bowl mix all the ingredients together, then cover with cling film and leave in a warm place at room temperature overnight.

Poolish ingredients	
Stiff starter	200g
Wholemeal rye flour	35g
Strong white flour	80g
Water	185g

Method: Day 2, morning

In a bowl mix all the ingredients together, cover the bowl and leave in a warm place until the evening. Ideally, the poolish will have at least six hours to stand.

Dough ingredients	
Poolish	500g
Strong white flour	650g
Fine salt	15g
Water	300g

Method: Day 2, evening

1. In the early evening, add the other ingredients to the poolish in the bowl and mix well to form a ragged and sticky dough. Cover the bowl and leave in a warm place for about one hour.

2. Fold the dough. Pull a section of the dough out to the side and fold it into the middle of the ball. Repeat this going around the ball of dough until you get back to the beginning (four or five folds). Use the scraper to turn the dough upside down, cover the bowl and leave for another 5–10 minutes.

3. Repeat this step three times. After the final fold, cover the bowl again and leave to rest for one hour at room temperature.

4. Turn the dough out of the bowl on to a lightly floured surface. Stretch out one side of the dough and fold it into the middle. Repeat this with each of the four 'sides' of the dough. Put the dough back in the bowl upside down and leave to rest for another hour at room temperature.

5. Stretch one side of the dough out and fold it into the middle. Repeat this all around the outside of the dough until you get back to your starting point. Flip it so the seam side is facing down. Use your left hand to hold the dough in place and your right hand to rotate the dough, tucking it under and tightening it as you go around. (If you are left-handed, you might want to use your right hand to stabilize and your left hand to rotate.) The idea here is to increase the strength of the dough without tearing it. The final surface of the dough should feel taut to the touch.

6. Dust a round banneton basket with flour. Turn the dough out on to a lightly floured work surface, then fold the top of the dough into the centre and tuck the sides into the centre. Now fold the bottom of the dough into the centre, leaving a seam in the dough. Place the dough into the loaf tin seam side down, and place this into the fridge for an overnight prove.

7. To test whether the dough has proved enough, press your finger about 2–3cm into it, then remove. If the dough pushes back out slowly, it is ready. If it springs back quickly, the dough is under-proved; if it does not spring back at all, it

is over-proved. If the dough is over-proved, you need to de-gas it, re-shape and prove again. Remember, the second attempt will take half the time to achieve the full prove.

8. Preheat the oven to 240°C/fan 230°C/gas mark 9. Place a roasting dish in the bottom of the oven to heat up, and a flat baking tray on one of the shelves. Fill a cup with water and place to one side ready to use.

9. When the oven is up to temperature, transfer the loaf tin on to the baking tray and place the tray in the oven. Pour the cup of water into the preheated roasting dish at the bottom. The moisture created will make the dough lighter, help to set the crust and give it a lovely sheen.

10. Turn the temperature down to 220°C/fan 210°C/gas mark 9 and bake for 30–35 minutes. To check if the bread is baked through, tap the bottom – it should sound hollow.

11. Allow to cool at room temperature for one hour.

• •

PAIN AU LEVAIN

Ingredients

Ingredients	
Sourdough starter	300g
Strong white bread flour	680g
Medium or dark rye flour	90g
Water	455g
Sea salt	15g

Method: Day 1

1. Add all the ingredients except the salt to a medium or large mixing bowl. Mix the dough with your hands or a dough whisk, until the ingredients are just incorporated. Cover the bowl with cling film and set aside in a warm area for 30 minutes. This is called the autolyse period, when the dough can incorporate all of the liquid.

2. Move the dough to the work surface and mix by hand for a few minutes, until it just comes together. Sprinkle the salt all over the dough and continue

hand mixing until it reaches a medium consistency. It should be somewhat silky to the touch. Place the dough into a lightly oiled container, cover, and leave to ferment for two hours total.

3. Pull a section of the dough out to the side and fold it into the middle of the ball. Repeat this going around the ball of dough until you get back to the beginning (four or five folds). Use the scraper to turn the dough upside down, cover the bowl and leave for another 5–10 minutes.

4. Repeat this step three times. After the final fold, cover the bowl again and leave to rest for one hour at room temperature.

5. Turn the dough out of the bowl on to a lightly floured surface. Stretch out one side of the dough and fold it into the middle. Repeat this with each of the four 'sides' of the dough. Put the dough back in the bowl upside down and leave to rest for another hour at room temperature.

6. Stretch one side of the dough out and fold it into the middle. Repeat this all around the outside of the dough until you get back to your starting point. Flip it so the seam side is facing down. Use your left hand to hold the dough in place and your right hand to rotate the dough, tucking it under and tightening it as you go around. (If you are left-handed, you might want to use your right hand to stabilize and your left hand to rotate.) The idea here is to increase the strength of the dough without tearing it. The final surface of the dough should feel taut to the touch.

7. Line a long banneton basket with flour, and turn out the dough on to a lightly floured work surface. Fold the top of the dough into the centre and tuck the sides into the centre, then fold the bottom of the dough into the centre, leaving a seam in the dough. Put the basket into the fridge for an overnight prove.

Method: Day 2

1. To test whether the dough has proved enough, press your finger about 2–3cm into it, then remove. If the dough pushes back out slowly, it is ready. If it springs back quickly, the dough is under-proved; if it does not spring back at all, it is over-proved. If

the dough is over-proved, you need to de-gas it, re-shape and prove again. Remember, the second attempt will take half the time to achieve the full prove.

2. Preheat the oven to 240°C/fan 230°C/gas mark 9. Place a roasting dish in the bottom of the oven to heat up, and a flat baking tray on one of the shelves. Fill a cup with water and place to one side ready to use.

3. When the oven is up to temperature, turn out the dough from the proofing basket and score the dough with a knife, allowing expansion of the dough through the oven spring process onto the baking tray, and place the tray in the oven. Pour the cup of water into the preheated roasting dish at the bottom. the moisture created will make the dough lighter, help to set the crust and give it a lovely sheen.

4. Turn the temperature down to 220°C/fan 210°C/gas mark 9 and bake for 30–35 minutes. To check if the bread is baked through, tap the bottom – it should sound hollow.

5. Allow to cool at room temperature for one hour.

ITALIAN BREADS

Italians have a high consumption of bread, eating just less than their neighbours in Germany. The bread eaten in Italy is predominantly white; this harks back to Roman times when white flour was reserved for the wealthier citizens, and the darker grain was sold on to the poor, along with rye and chestnut flour, which made pane nero, darker-coloured bread. Right up there with white flour is durum wheat or semolina. Following the fall of the Roman Empire, artisan bread-makers began to experiment with local ingredients and the resulting breads took on regional changes; by the time of the Renaissance, many of today's regional breads had become well established. There are regional differences in most countries, but nowhere are they defended more fiercely than in Italy – every Italian citizen believes that their version is correct and the best!

One of the oldest known breads that is still baked today is pane di padula, which is produced in the province of Salerno, Campania. It is made from a mixture of wheat flour and semolina, and, before baking, the top of the loaf is engraved with squares, which are said to resemble the Pompeii mosaics.

The Italians' preferred method of pre-ferment is called 'biga', a thick dough that varies from 45 to 60% hydration and is very similar to a stiff starter.

Visually speaking, the majority of the Italian breads do not match the finishing techniques of the French breads, but this does not mean that they fail to deliver a fantastic flavour experience.

Marocca di Casola

An ancient bread typical of one small rural area (Casola, Lunigiana) in northern Italy. It is made almost entirely with chestnut flour.

MAROCCA DI CASOLA

Ingredients

Chestnut flour	350g
All-purpose flour	150g
Sourdough starter	150g
Water	220g
Salt	10g
Mashed potato	80g
Semolina	20g

Method: Day 1

Add all the ingredients into a bowl apart from the salt, mashed potato and semolina, combine together and fully incorporate. Leave at room temperature overnight covered with cling film.

Method: Day 2

1. Add the salt and knead for five minutes until gluten structure is developed. Leave to rest for 30 minutes.

2. Turn the dough out on to a work surface and gently fold in the potato. The dough will feel firm and will not have the natural sticky characteristics of a sourdough.

3. Shape into a boule and place on to a baking tray with a dusting of semolina.

4. Cover with cling film and leave for two hours to prove at room temperature.
5. Turn the proved dough out onto an inverted, preheated baking dish, make one slash in the centre, and bake in a preheated oven for 30–35 minutes. To check if the bread is baked through, tap the bottom – it should sound hollow.
6. Allow to cool at room temperature for one hour before eating.

• •

Pagnotta del Dittaino

The dittaino loaf is produced in Sicily with durum wheat. It is a round loaf with an incredibly tasty crust that hides a compact, uniform crumb, with an unmistakable taste and softness.

Pandoro

The pandoro is a traditional Christmas bread from Verona that is considered to be a viennoiserie. Its name means 'bread of gold', reflecting its pleasing yellow colour, which comes from the huge number of eggs that are included.

Pane di Patate della Garfagnana

Also known as 'garfagnino', this bread is part of an ancient tradition that replaces part of the flour with potato, in order to make up for a poor wheat harvest. It then survived over the centuries to become a speciality of the Garfagnana area.

• •

PANE DI PATATE DELLA GARFAGNANA

Ingredients	
Sourdough starter	400g
Plain, unbleached flour	1kg
Water	350g
Boiled mashed potato	200g
Salt	8g
Extra virgin olive oil (for greasing)	

Method: Day 1
1. Add into a mixing bowl the sourdough starter, the flour, half of the water and the salt. Mix all the ingredients, then add the remaining water gradually. Knead for six to eight minutes until you get a smooth dough. Do not over-mix, as the weak flour will not tolerate a long kneading.
2. Let the dough rest for about half an hour in a bowl greased with extra virgin olive oil.
3. Pull a section of the dough out to the side and fold it into the middle of the ball. Repeat this going around the ball of dough until you get back to the beginning (four or five folds). Use the scraper to turn the dough upside down, cover the bowl and leave for another 5–10 minutes.
4. Repeat this step three times. After the final fold, cover the bowl again and leave to rest for one hour at room temperature.
5. Turn the dough out of the bowl on to a lightly floured surface. Stretch out one side of the dough and fold it into the middle. Repeat this with each of the four 'sides' of the dough. Put the dough back in the bowl upside down and leave to rest for another hour at room temperature.
6. Turn the dough out again, then stretch one side out and fold it into the middle. Repeat this all around the outside of the dough until you get back to your starting point. Flip it so the seam side is facing down. Use your left hand to hold the dough in place and your right hand to rotate the dough, tucking it under and tightening it as you go around. (If you are left-handed, you might want to use your right hand to stabilize and your left hand to rotate.) The idea here is to increase the strength of the dough without tearing it. The final surface of the dough should feel taut to the touch.
7. Line a round banneton basket with flour and turn out the dough on to a lightly floured work surface.
8. Fold the top of the dough into the centre and tuck the sides into the centre, then fold the

bottom of the dough into the centre, leaving a seam. Put the basket into the fridge for an overnight prove.

Method: Day 2

1. To test whether the dough has proved enough, press your finger about 2–3cm into it, then remove. If the dough pushes back out slowly, it is ready. If it springs back quickly, the dough is under-proved; if it does not spring back at all, it is over-proved. If the dough is over-proved, you need to de-gas it, re-shape and prove again. Remember, the second attempt will take half the time to achieve the full prove.

2. Preheat the oven to 240°C/fan 230°C/gas mark 9. Place a roasting dish in the bottom of the oven to heat up, and a flat baking tray on one of the shelves. Fill a cup with water and place to one side ready to use.

3. When the oven is up to temperature, turn out the dough from the proofing basket and score the dough with a knife, allowing expansion of the dough through the oven spring process onto the baking tray, and place the tray in the oven. Pour the cup of water into the preheated roasting dish at the bottom. The moisture created will make the dough lighter, help to set the crust and give it a lovely sheen.

4. Turn the temperature down to 220°C/fan 210°C/gas mark 9 and bake for 30–35 minutes. To check if the bread is baked through, tap the bottom – it should sound hollow.

5. Allow to cool at room temperature for one hour.

● ●

PANDORO

Dough 1 ingredients

Sourdough starter	120g
Water	90g
Strong white bread flour	190g

Dough 2 ingredients

Dough 1	315g
Water at 105–110°C	60g
Sourdough starter	60g
Strong white bread flour	345g
Large eggs	3
Sugar	6 tbsps
After proving	
Honey	85g
Large eggs	12
Vanilla extract	3 tbsps
Vanilla bean paste	1 tbsp
Large egg yolks	6
Sugar	465g
Butter, very soft	60g
Icing sugar for dusting	

Dough 3 ingredients

Cocoa butter	60g
Unsalted butter	550g
Bread flour	540g
Salt	1½ tsps
Almond flour	300g

A note about timing: if you start at 9am the day before you bake, you will be mixing the final dough at 5pm. To bake the following morning, the start can be shifted to later. For example, if you start at 12 noon, you will be mixing the final dough at 8pm.

A couple of sample timelines might look like the following:

Timeline 1

9am	Start dough 1
1pm	Start dough 2
5pm	Start dough 3
6am	Bake

Timeline 2

12pm	Start dough 1
4pm	Start dough 2
8pm	Start dough 3
9am	Bake

The method below follows Timeline 1.

Method: Dough 1, about 9am

1. To make dough 1, mix together by hand the sourdough starter, the water and the first part of the bread flour. Knead it until you get a smooth ball of dough.
2. Place in a small bowl, cover with cling film and leave to rise for four hours. The dough should be puffed up and doubled in size. You will not need all of this dough; some of it will inevitably be thrown out when you measure the quantities for the second dough.

Method: Dough 2, about 1pm

1. To make dough 2, stir the sourdough starter into the water and leave to stand for 5 minutes. It should start to bubble.
2. Measure out the amount of dough 1 that you need (315g). Discard the rest or reserve it for another project.
3. Break up the measured-out sourdough into several chunks and add them to the flour in a mixing bowl. Add the yeast, the three eggs and the sugar. Knead until you get a very smooth ball of dough. It will take about 5 to 8 minutes and some hard work to get it smooth, but it will happen eventually.
4. Place in a large bowl and cover with cling film. Leave to rise again for three to four hours, or until the dough has quadrupled in size.
5. To get ready for mixing the final dough, take four 12-cup pandoro moulds, or a bundt pan (most of which also have 12 cups). A spiral fluted one would look good. Using very soft, room-temperature butter, take a pastry brush and make sure all the nooks and crannies are coated before flouring the moulds. Put to one side.

Method: Dough 3, about 5pm

1. To make dough 3, melt the cocoa butter in the microwave until barely melted. Be careful – it will get very hot. Leave it to cool for a bit, but do not allow to become completely cold.
2. In a mixer, whip the butter until it is light and fluffy. With the mixer still running, pour in the slightly cooled cocoa butter in a steady stream. Continue to whip until the butter is light in colour and doubled in volume. Scrape it out and set aside. You can wipe out the remaining butter but there is no need to clean the bowl.
3. Into the mixing bowl, stir together the flour and salt.
4. Return to dough 2, which has now risen, and divide it into five or so pieces. Add the pieces to the dough 3 flour mixture, along with nine of the eggs and the honey.
5. Knead this dough mixture for 6 to 7 minutes until the dough is smooth, cleans the sides of the bowl and is elastic. Add in the remaining three eggs and knead until incorporated.
6. Add three egg yolks, vanilla, and vanilla bean paste. To prevent splashing, start the mixer at low speed, then turn up to medium after the egg yolks have begun to mix in. Beat until the egg has been completely incorporated.
7. Add in the remaining three egg yolks and again mix until incorporated. The dough may take a while to mix completely. Have faith and continue to beat, scraping down the bowl and pushing the dough off the paddle where necessary.
8. Turn the mixer down to a low speed again, and beat in half of the sugar. Add the remaining sugar and beat until the dough is very smooth.
9. Now add half of the beaten butter mixture from dough 3. Again, beat until it has been incorporated. Repeat with the remaining butter.
10. Add the almond flour and beat until the dough is very smooth and fully incorporated. This is the final step.

Method: Final rising, about 6pm

1. Divide the dough between the four buttered moulds, using scales to ensure the division is even. As the dough is almost pourable, you may find it is easier just to accept that it will be messy, and use your hands to divide and move dough between the moulds as you weigh them. The dough will look like it will never get to the top of the moulds, but it will eventually quadruple in size.

2. Cover the filled moulds loosely with cling film and leave to rise for 11 to 12 hours.

Method: Baking, about 5am

1. The pandoros will have risen to the top of the moulds and have domed slightly over. After one hour, carefully remove the cling film. Some of the dough from the top may stick to it, but this is not a problem.
2. At this point, preheat the oven to 350°C/gas mark 10. If you are doing this overnight, you can go back to bed for a nap for 45 minutes to an hour. Leave the oven to preheat completely for at least 30 minutes.
3. Bake the pandoros for 40 to 50 minutes. The pandoro will be very golden brown, and the centre will look like it has fallen slightly. This is normal. The best way of seeing whether they are done is to use an instant-read thermometer, to check when they reach 205–210°C fan/gas mark 6.
4. Let the baked pandoros rest in the moulds for 20 minutes, and then unmould and leave to cool completely.
5. Serve generously, dusted in powdered sugar if desired. If the bread has been baked in a bundt pan, it can be cut into wedges or sliced from the top to create 'stars'.
6. Last step: enjoy the sense of achievement that you have as you eat the results of all your hard work!

• •

AMERICAN AND BRITISH BREADS

Historically, British bakers were using superb indigenous flours such as emmer, einkorn, spelt and barley, and they would have been well aware of making bread with a wild yeast culture. However, since the middle of the twentieth century onwards, British baking has become more closely associated with the Chorleywood Process, the method used for the mass production of a tasteless, homogenous, consistent loaf with a long shelf life. There is still time for a recovery, though, and as a baker from Britain I am doing my best to help to restore the nation's reputation in the world of breads and baking.

What can be said about American breads? Although America is a relatively young country, it is quite similar in some respects to Britain. They are both societies that have a long tradition of welcoming the migration of people from other places, creating the perfect environment for the growth of new ideas. When people come together from all corners of the world, and a fusion of all traditions is thrown into one mixing bowl, bakers can take ideas from that bowl and create something wonderful and new.

The Americans and British may not have a sourdough history that goes back thousands of years, but both countries are making massive efforts to improve, particularly America. The baking world cannot underestimate the impact that America has had on the perception of what 'good bread' tastes or looks like, and it all started in California.

The culture of California is tied to the culture of the United States as a whole. However, there are features that are unique to this particular state. With roots in the cultures of Spain, Asia, Mexico and the eastern United States, California integrates foods, languages and traditions from all over the world. The California Gold Rush of the 1850s is still seen as a symbol of California's modern economic style, a pioneering spirit that tends to generate technology. It was at about this time that new ideas and technologies began to kick-start the development of sourdough bread in San Francisco. A little over a century later, the hippie movement began in that same city; when it comes to bread, this is the period when everything changed again. The subsequent rise in the development of artisan bakeries, in the 1980s, strongly influenced what has been called the 'Bread Revolution'.

The artisan bread movement represented a return to low-volume production of handmade loaves. It was, in some ways, a return to older techniques, but in other ways it was also a shift, to French and Italian techniques. The new artisan breads were very crusty. Loaves were exposed to steam while baking (a technique developed in Vienna, Austria), creating a shiny surface that could be crusty or chewy, while keeping the interior moist. 'Rustic' breads used wholegrain flours, including rye flour and wholewheat. Breads were scored with decorative cross-cuts, along which the bread cracked while rising and baking to allow the crust to expand. The scoring of the loaves was in a distinctive style, which identified each bakery.

SWEDISH BREADS

In recent years, sourdough bread has become popular in Sweden, with many new bakeries specializing in it. Interestingly, Swedes have tended to buy bread supplied by industrial bakeries – research carried out for the EU in 2011 showed that about three-quarters of the bread bought by Swedes was pre-packed and only a quarter was freshly baked – so business was always tough for small bakeries. It was almost exactly the opposite of the situation in France or Italy. Artisan bakers in Sweden were getting only a tiny slice of the market; indeed, within Europe, only Estonia and Ireland bought less bread from artisan bakeries.

Fortunately, the situation has been improving in recent years. Although there has been a decline in bread consumption generally across Sweden, the quality has improved and new bakeries have emerged. Generally, in Sweden, across all foodstuffs, there has been an increase in demand for natural and healthier products, so the demand for good sourdough bread has steadily increased.

Of course, sourdough bread in Sweden is fairly similar to sourdough anywhere else, with levains and baguettes being particularly popular, but a few differences do stand out. Rye is widely used, and bread in Sweden is more often flavoured with additions such as aniseed, caraway or fennel than in the UK. Artisan bakers in Sweden also tend to follow the seasons more. The following ingredients are some popular seasonal flavourings:

Spring
Nässlor (nettles)
Anis (aniseed)
Gräslök (chives)
Grön sparris (green asparagus)
Valnötter (walnuts)

Summer
Rabarber (rhubarb)
Potatis med kummin och dill (potatoes with caraway and dill)

Autumn
Äpplen (apples)
Pumpa (pumpkin)
Lingon (lingonberries)

Winter
Saffran (saffron)
Vört (wort)

Much of the increased popularity of sourdough bread can be attributed to the work of Sweden's most famous baker, Jan Hedh. He runs a bakery and café, Olof Viktors, in Glemmingebro, near the coastal town of Ystad in southern Sweden. Despite being rather secluded, his bakery contributes massively to the Swedish bread community. Jan is deeply knowledgeable and a real craftsman who uses wood-fired brick ovens. Not only does he try to maintain traditional Swedish recipes and techniques, but he has also been responsible for the training of a new generation of talented bakers.

Sourdough baking is not something reserved just for professionals. Such is the contemporary popularity of baking sourdough at home in Sweden, that rich Swedes can even check in their sourdegskultur to a hotel at Stockholm's Arlanda Airport for someone to look after it whilst they are away!

RUSSIAN BREADS

Russia has a wide range of hearty sourdough 'black breads' that are deep in colour and rich in taste. One of the most popular is borodinsky, a traditional dark-brown sourdough loaf made of rye and wheat flour, with a pinch of sweet molasses or honey and spicy coriander. Every Russian citizen is familiar with the taste of this bread, and it is the subject of a beautiful but sorrowful legend. When, in 1812, Russian General Alexander Tuchkov perished at the Battle of Borodino, his heartbroken widow ordered the building of a convent at the site of the bloody battle with the French. Some believe the convent's nuns came up with the recipe for the bread, which was initially called 'memorial' and was later named after the fateful battle. The bread's dark colour allegedly represents mourning and grief, and the coriander seeds symbolize bullets and grapeshot.

A whole book could easily be dedicated to the range of sourdough breads that can be found throughout the world. Be a recipe hunter and enrich your knowledge as a baker. It is a wonderful thing to re-visit the classics from your own past – like that milk loaf that your grandmother used to make – but do not limit yourself to what you know, or what feels safe. Go out and explore. There is a whole world of sourdough out there just waiting to be discovered!

CHAPTER 8

TROUBLESHOOTING GUIDE AND TOP TIPS

Making and producing sourdough products can be a daunting process, even to the professional baker. This guide reflects on some of the questions that I have been asked over the years. In the early days, I had to research some of the answers and perform experiments to discover the best response, but hopefully the following will help you to troubleshoot in most situations.

'Why is there no movement in my starter?'
Signs of movement, volume and bubbles are related first and foremost to the environment in which the starter is kept. A temperature of around 32°C (89.6°F) encourages growth of the yeast, but yeast will stop growing at 35–37°C (95–99°F), so it is a good idea to keep a thermometer close. Remember, the outside temperature will affect movement in the starter; for example, a cold snap in winter could result in it being sluggish. When bringing the starter from the fridge to room temperature, place a rubber band around the jar, to indicate the volume; this will give a visual aid to enable you to follow the starter's progress as it grows and expands.

'How do I know if my starter is dead?'
It takes a lot to kill a starter, as they tend to be very resilient. However, there are occasions when they are not revivable. The main causes of death are cross-contamination of bad bacteria and/or too much heat. It will be apparent if it is dead, as it will smell of dirty nappies. Throw it away and start again; in six days you will be able to have another go at baking.

'What if my starter has mould on it?'
Mould can appear if the starter has been contaminated with undesirable bacteria due to cross-contamination; this can happen, for example, when using a spoon already used for something else. If mould is visible in the starter it is best practice to discard the whole lot and start again. Unlike cheese-making, mould is not a good thing to have in a sourdough starter.

'I can see dark liquid on top of my sourdough starter.'
This is a natural occurrence when the starter has produced an alcohol substance commonly known as hooch. This is an indicator that it is hungry and needs to be fed, and usually occurs if the starter has been kept in direct sunlight or in a warm environment. First, place the starter in a cooler environment. Then there are two options: you can simply discard all the hooch, or just discard a little and stir the rest into the starter prior to a refresher feed. For the refresher feed, add 50g of the starter's original flour and 50g of water, but this time drop in a teaspoon of honey too. The yeast will be rapidly invigorated by the sugar. Leave the starter again with a loose cover on top in an ideal temperature, and monitor for around 12 hours. Next time you look, the starter should be perky, active and alive.

'Can I speed up the revival of a sluggish sourdough starter by putting it in the oven?'
Warmth does aid the fermentation process, so putting the starter in the oven would in theory reinvigorate the

yeast bacteria. However, the yeast will be killed once the oven temperature reaches 140°C. Sourdough is a slow food and not to be rushed. The proper sour taste is created over time, so a quick bolt in the oven is not appropriate. If you want a quick fix, baking sourdough may not be for you!

'Can I freeze my starter?'
Yes, you can. The yeast bacteria will lie dormant in this state. When bringing it out of the freezer, take it out a few days before you want to use it, initially placing it in the fridge to defrost. After around 12 hours, take it out and give it a refresher feed of 50g of the starter's original flour along with 50g of water and 3g of honey. This will aid the yeast in its recovery, as it will feed from the additional sugar provided.

'My starter is ten years old. I use it regularly but want to reserve some in case of disaster.'
To dry some starter for storing, take a piece of baking parchment and spread on to it a thin layer of the original sourdough starter. Lift this on to a baking tray and pop into the oven, using only the oven light to aid in the drying process; this is a drying process, not a baking process. Once it has dried, take it out of the oven, break into a pestle and mortar, and grind gently into a powder, then pop into a Ziplock bag and label it. This can then be kept in your cupboard until you need to use it; it should last indefinitely.

'I've been feeding it regularly and now I have a very large Tupperware of starter, what can I do with it?'
You can gift this to a friend along with instructions on how to use and maintain it. Alternatively, you can freeze some, just in case. As a last resort, pour some down the drain and keep around 600g in the fridge.

'How long do I need to feed it before using it to bake with?'
Take your starter out of the fridge the day before using it and feed it, leaving it out overnight at room temperature. If you want to make sure you are using it at its optimum, do this at a time when you can observe it and use it just as it peaks. This will be different for

every starter, depending upon room temperature and the acidity levels. To check whether it is ready to use for baking, drop a spoonful of starter into a cup of warm water; if it floats, it is good to go, as it is now producing carbon dioxide bubbles. If it sinks, it needs to be left for longer.

'My sourdough looks flat.'
There could be a number of reasons for this. First, your starter may not be active enough, so you need to make sure you are using it at its most potent. To be aware of your starter's behaviour, watch it when it has been fed and left at room temperature, checking it every hour or so. Once it has bubbled to its maximum height and just dropped, it is ready to be used.

Ensure that a good gluten structure has developed. To determine whether the dough has been kneaded enough, try the window-pane test. (Can you stretch out a small piece of dough between your fingers and thumb to form a translucent 'window' without it tearing?)

Another possibility is that it has been over-proved. Again, watch your dough. It will peak in its rise and after this it will drop and spread.

'I can't tell when my bread is proved.'
This is something that comes with time and practice. When you think it looks ready, gently press your thumb into the dough. If the indentation stays there (or springs back very slowly), it is ready for the oven.

'My slashes don't open.'
There are many different reasons for this, but one solution is to use a Dutch oven – it works every time.

'Why don't I get the big holes?'
Mainly, you need to ensure you are using a sufficiently wet dough – one with high hydration levels – and that you use the stretch and fold method throughout the first rise to strengthen the gluten; high hydration plus lamination gives aeration.

'Why is my crust really dull?'
This is down to steam. Either spray the oven immediately when you put the bread in or, if using

a Dutch oven, make sure this is preheated first, then remove it from the oven with oven gloves, lower the dough into the pot and put back into the oven with the lid on. Remove the lid 10–15 minutes before the end of the bake to get the desired shiny dark brown crust.

'A collection of mistakes'.

CHAPTER 9

CONCLUSION

You should now be fully equipped to make, develop, and experiment with the many different methods of sourdough-making, flour incorporation and flavouring techniques. The most important asset when working with sourdough, whether it is being made for pleasure, mass production, or out of pure curiosity, is patience. If you are to achieve those Instagram-perfect sourdough bubbles, you need careful attention to the recipe and equal attention to the needs of your starter.

REFERENCES

BIBLIOGRAPHY

Gobbetti, M., Rizzelo, C.G., Di Cagno, R., and De Angelis, M., 'How the sourdough may affect the functional features of leavened baked goods', *Food Microbiology*, (February 2014, 37, pages 30-40)

Poutanen, K., Flander, L. and Katina, K., 'Sourdough and cereal fermentation in a nutritional perspective', *Food Microbial*, VTT Technical Research Centre of Finland, (October 2009)

RECOMMENDED FURTHER READING

Blake, A. and Collister, L., *The Bread Book: A Step-by-Step Guide to Making over 130 Delicious Breads*, Conran Octopus, 1994

Jones, M., Gellaty, L. and Gellaty, J., *Baking School: The Bread Ahead Cookbook*, Penguin, 2017

Lepard, D., *The Handmade Loaf*, Octopus Publishing Group Ltd. 2017

Myhrvold, N. and Migoya, F., *Modernist Cuisine: Modernist Bread*, The Cooking Lab, 2017

Oritz, J., *The Village Baker: Classic Regional Breads from Europe and America*, Ten Speed Press, 1997

Reinhart, P., *The Bread Baker's Apprentice: Mastering the Art of Extraordinary Bread*, Ten Speed Press, 2001

Robertson, C., *Tartine Bread*, Chronicle Books LLC, 2010

CONVERSION CHARTS

Weight

UK/Metric	US/Imperial
15g	½oz
30g	1oz
60g	2oz
115g	¼lb
150g	⅓lb
225g	½lb
300g	⅔lb
350g	¾lb
450g	1lb

Volume

1 teaspoon (tsp) = 0.17fl oz = 4.93 ml

1 tablespoon (tbsp) = 0.52fl oz = 14.79 ml

UK/Metric	Imperial	US
2.5ml		½ tsp
5ml		1 tsp
15ml	½fl oz	1 tbsp
60ml	2fl oz	¼ cup
90ml	2.7fl oz	⅓ cup
120ml	4fl oz	½ cup
180ml	6fl oz	¾ cup
240ml	8fl oz/½pt	1 cup
480ml	16fl oz/1pt	2 cups

Temperature

(0°C × 9/5) + 32 = 32°F

Degrees centigrade (°C)	Degrees Fahrenheit (°F)	Gas mark
1°C	33°F	
2°C	35°F	
3°C	37°F	
4°C	39°F	
5°C	41°F	
100°C	210°F	
110°C	230°F	¼
120°C	250°F	
130°C	265°F	½
140°C	285°F	1
150°C	300°F	2
160°C	320°F	
170°C	340°F	3
180°C	355°F	4
190°C	375°F	5
200°C	390°F	6
210°C	410°F	
220°C	430°F	7
230°C	445°F	8
240°C	465°F	9
250°C	480°F	

RECIPE INDEX

INDEX